I AM ONLY HUMAN

I AM ONLY HUMAN

BETWEEN EXPECTATIONS AND REALITY, THE TRAGEDY OF MODERN LIFE

Georgi Danov

Georgi Danov

1

CONTENTS

Preamble	3
Introduction	6
Chapter 1 - Irrationality	11

Section One - It is All About the Ego

Chapter 2 - Ego	31
Chapter 3 – Superiority Illusion	40
Chapter 4 – Cognitive Dissonance Reduction	52
Chapter 5 – Self-Handicapping	59

Section Two - Brain and Heuristics

Chapter 6 – Cognition and Jumping to Conclusions	67
Chapter 7 – Narratives and Conclusions on Steroids	76

Chapter 8 – Judging a Book by the Cover — 84
Chapter 9 – Snap Decisions and Prejudice — 92
Chapter 10 – We Only See Black and White — 105

Section Three - It is All Coming Together

Chapter 11 – Perceiving the World Differently — 116
Chapter 12 – Attitudes and Attitude Change — 126
Chapter 13 – Willpower — 142
Chapter 14 – Failure and Blame — 154
Chapter 15 – Social Comparisons — 165
Chapter 16 – Selling Happiness — 173
Chapter 17 – Fear of Change and the Status Quo — 181
Chapter 18 – Greed — 200
Conclusion — 219
Notes — 225
References — 229

2

Preamble

Hi, my name is Georgi. Nice to meet you, Reader! You probably wonder what this book is all about. Let me tell you – it is about me, it is about you, it is also about all people who often feel overwhelmed and constantly playing catch up with everything and everyone. It is about all of us who feel like we can never meet all the expectations and pressure of the modern way of life despite how hard we try.

I live in London, one of the biggest and most vibrant cities in the world, the capital of a country, which has shaped the modern way of life – a cradle of capitalism, mother of the industrial revolution, once a global empire, and as a result a melting pot of every culture and nationality under the Sun. And I will tell you one thing – living here is tiring. Like many of my fellow Londoners, I spend hours every day commuting to work, busting my a** to stay on top of my mortgage/rent payments and bills, while competing with millions of smart and ambitious people in this capitalist, money-making machine to build a career. And this is while also trying to stay relatively fit and healthy, have enough time for my family and friends, compete with everyone else on social media, and somehow remain sane in the whole hustle and bustle. But this is not just me. While London takes everything up a notch, this is the reality for most people around the world these days. Unless you are one of those very fortunate but very few people, born with a silver spoon in their mouths, you know what I am talking about.

Every time in history has had its specific challenges - wars, diseases, poverty, financial and economic meltdowns, people before us have not had it easy either. We probably have it easier than every generation before us in a comparative perspective. Not that we have none of these today, but globally we probably live in the most stable times compared to any period before. And yet, we face unique set of challenges, which characterise our time. We try to be everything, do everything, and meet the ever-growing expectations of the society we live in. The revolutions in technology, communications, transport, and social media have uncovered an endless sea of opportunities and created endless expectations. We try to stay constantly connected and informed; we try to be the best we can in every field, we try to keep our minds open and liberal, we try to live up to our own and others' expectations. We cannot!

Throughout this book, I will look at some of the most common traits of our characters, shortcomings, and natural proclivities, which often stay in the way of achieving all this. This is not because I dislike the world or doubt our ability to learn, adapt and evolve. As a species, we have proved time and time again that we can. I am writing this book hoping that by shining light on some of our shortcomings and limitations, I would add a little dose of reality to what we all should expect of ourselves and others. Because, despite all of our strengths and successes, we are, and we will always remain, only humans.

Finally, before we proceed, I wanted to address the obvious question – who am I to write this book? Why would I think I know anything about us as humans, and what we can or cannot do? The simple answer is – I am no one. But, this is what makes my message powerful. We do not need an accomplished political, entrepreneurial, or scientific figure to tell us what to expect or not from their position of authority or relative remoteness of the issues, worries and struggles of everyday people. Like every other in this world, I am just a human, and this is just my ordinary take on ordinary people's lives. I have tried to convey my views in a simple and relatable manner, with humour here and there, and most important, with a huge dose of humility and sincerity, because like you, I am only human.

3

Introduction

In 1963, the Bronx Zoo introduced a curious exhibit, which indubitably garnered visitors' attention. It was labelled "The most dangerous animal in the world." Turns out, it was a mirror! Underneath, there was another interesting sign reading, "You are looking at the most dangerous animal in the world. It alone of all the animals that ever lived can exterminate (and has) entire species of animals. Now it has the power to wipe out all life on earth."

Sixty years later, this statement continues to resonate with many people. Its power has only grown! But, let's dig deeper into another curious element of the label – we were called animals. We are, even though some may argue otherwise. As humans, we have consciousness, we have restraint, we are capable of rational thought, and we can envision ourselves in the future and thinking abstractly… impelling some of us to contend that we are far more superior to animals. These statements are not devoid of truth, but an honest introspection would reveal we have a lot more in common with animals and our primal ancestors than we would care to (or like to!) admit.

If we look back at everything we have achieved as a species, from fragile inhabitants of the African savannah to where we are now, and all we can do today, our journey has been nothing short of spectacular. Our accomplishments become even more staggering when we realize that much of the progress we have made has accelerated through the 20th and early 21st centuries. Technologically and culturally, the world has changed a lot more in the last 200 years than it did for 10,000 years before that. If we generally accept that the first Homo sapiens appeared 300 000 years ago, it took us 300 000 - 118 years to fly in the skies, when the Wright brothers invented the first plane in 1903. The flight lasted just 12 seconds.

Mere 58 years later, Yuri Gagarin not only took to the skies but also went into space. Likewise, it took us 300 000 - 85 years to create the first computer (Alan Turing 1936). It can be safely concluded that over the past 85 years, computers pretty much control our lives today, having permeated everything we do daily. Add the automobile (which didn't become a practical way of transportation until the 20th century despite being invented in the late 19th century), the light bulb, nuclear power, penicillin and antibiotics, television, the internet, and so much more. This technological revolution has inexorably brought about a gamut of educational, scientific, cultural, and social changes, which shape the world as we know it today.

Often, our brains and bodies simply cannot keep up with the pace and intensity of these changes. Paradoxically, we live in a world where everyone, including you and me, is increasingly demanding more. That's right. The technological explosion has created countless possibilities, but also countless expectations, which go hand-in-hand.

We are supposed to live in the most liberal, permissive, and accommodating time the world has ever seen. We are supposed to be free, happy, satisfied with what we have. In many ways, we really are. Yet, we also live in a time, which is more mentally and psychologically challenging than any other before that. Given everything we have achieved and the comfort of the 21st century, it sounds counter-intuitive that, in some ways, we have regressed as a society – both emotionally and psychologically. We are not generally happier than our ancestors were a hundred or five hundred years ago.

More people suffer from stress and stress-related diseases today than in previous centuries, which is especially prevalent among the youth. We try to do too much, to do a few things at a time, to stay constantly connected, to absorb an endless influx of information, to conform to countless societal norms and pressures. There is an incredible amount of pressure on women to be pretty and fit into society's definitions and norms of beauty; on men to be successful and wealthy; on children to take on a countless number of courses and activities to fulfil their parents' own unfulfilled ambitions; and generally, on anyone to act rational, to be always liberal and understanding, to effectively disregard a lot of the very feelings and emotions which make us human. Astonishing as we are, here's a truth we would do well to come to terms with: we are not equipped to meet the never-ending expectations of society and our own.

We, as humans, have conquered the land, the sea, and the sky; we have tremendous power over the processes and lives of everything and everyone else in the world. We are capable of incredible feats. Yet, despite our greatness, we also have a long list of shortcomings and limitations. We are egoistic and irrational, our decision making and judgment are far from being infallible, we are quick to judge others, we have a proclivity to egregiously repeat our mistakes, we fail to consider the underlying complexity of the world, and most importantly, we have a massive blind spot for these. To be fair, there are various reasons for that. Each one of us is, after all, a unique by-product of millions of years of evolution, cultural, environmental, and social factors. Taken together, they make us what we are. These are limitations, we hardly ever ruminate upon, do not fully understand, conveniently ignore, or deliberately develop selective amnesia for. This is understandable because all of the above help us perpetuate the illusion of our own infallibility and greatness, which are paramount for our inner peace if we function as normal beings. Yet, that doesn't make it true.

I am writing this book as an apologist for humanity. This is not because we are unworthy, unsuccessful, and generally bad people, but because we have grown to expect too much of everything and everyone to conform to various pressures of society and the so-called modern way of life. It does not matter if we believe we are the result of Darwinian evolution or a Godly creation. We came to exist and are a combination of good and bad, success and failure, strengths and weaknesses. In the following chapters, I will cover some of the most common shortcomings and ugly sides of our psyche, not because I do not believe in our capacity to be better, to do, and achieve more. Quite the opposite. Throughout history, we have demonstrated countless times that we are capable of extraordinary feats and achievements. But the fact of the matter remains that we are far from perfect as a society. For better or for worse, we are only humans. The sooner we accept the bad, the sooner can we start living a happier life and enjoy the good.

Well, let's read on. I hope you enjoy the book and will find it useful by the end unless you have dropped it because you are too smart already and there is nothing more you could learn. For this, I cannot blame you, as you are only human.

Chapter 1 - Irrationality

"We cannot reason ourselves out of our basic irrationality. All we can do is to learn the art of being irrational in a reasonable way."

- Aldous Huxley

As you can see, based on the first chapter of this book, I have picked the topic of (ir)rationality. It is a simpler topic, which will help us ease into the spirit and essence of this book. Yet, it remains one of the most salient chapters because it creates a framework to understand many subsequent chapters. This is the not-so-rational part about rationality – we do have an inkling of sorts about the reality that humans are not perfectly rational. Yet, we expect them to act rationally and inexorably annoyed upon realising this is not the case for some inexplicable reason. Furthermore, laws and regulations are written on the premise that people act rationally, thus not quite deciphering the essence of the human side. Traditional economic theory has been relentlessly criticised for overstating rationality as a concept and not observing how people behave. This explains why disciplines like behavioural economics and behavioural finance have become increasingly popular over the past couple of decades alone. More recently, we saw another poignant example of this in the UK and worldwide, amid the all-pervasive COVID pandemic. In May 2020, the UK government decided to ease the COVID lockdown, supposedly based on "good British common sense." I am a little perplexed about the irony or unintended humour (or both) in this outlandish assumption that belies common sense and deserves comeuppance. Just think about this: we spent two months in lockdown when not being able to go out drinking was ostensibly the biggest crisis facing mankind, but the government counted on people's common sense to avoid mass gatherings and stay safe? Needless to say, the striking episodes from popular places and areas in London, immediately following this, revealed a completely different story. And, rightly so. Of course, it wasn't just the UK that followed this approach. Many other countries in the world did the same and achieved the same end result. But, it is easy for me to say that after the effect. As I will discuss later in the book, we are very good at explaining events after the effect, not predicting them.

The problem with rationality is that it requires a few things to work – people acting in their long-term interest, emotional detachment, perfect knowledge, and sound reasoning, among other things. In real life, these are hard to come by. We are too often swayed by emotions, sentiments, and past experiences, which dramatically affect how we think and behave. Nor do we possess perfect knowledge to weigh all the pros and cons of our actions, or those of others. We do not always see the world as it is, but rather how we want it to be. Consider the following statements:

Statement 1: I am a rational human being.
Statement 2: I know when I am acting out of emotion and can control it.
Statement 3: I can rationally assess a situation and know when my thought process is influenced by other factors.

Have you ever given a thought to any of these three statements? I have, which brings me back to an earlier point – I am perfectly aware that, as a human, I am irrational, yet I often think I am not, while simultaneously scratching my head in disbelief at the behaviours and actions of others. I bet I am not the only one under this delusion. We all are not impervious to such situations and experiences in life. This takes us to a very important point for this chapter – we only consider rational what we can explicate or justify in our heads. We love narratives- little stories, which we keep telling ourselves to rationalise our irrationality. And if there is one thing we are particularly good at, it is inventing stories. This makes "because" an extremely powerful word. It really does not matter what kind of bull**** story we will concoct in our heads to justify our actions, as long as we can depend on a "because." I know many people would probably quickly dismiss it as "it might apply to others, not me", but before you do, just look at some very simple, everyday examples from our lives.

Example 1 – I don't really need this, I will buy it

Let me start with myself. If I give examples of irrationality, it only makes sense to start with my own experience. I have no qualms in admitting that I am just as irrational as everyone else. As I commence writing on this chapter, we have just gone into the first COVID lockdown, and I am one of the more fortunate people to work from home. And like most people doing that, I find that it works out pretty well financially, notwithstanding the occasional bouts of frustration and disturbing emotions. This is because I can't go out and spend it on drinks, dinners, and whatever else I usually do socially. At the same time, I got engaged to the love of my life. You are probably thinking, *'well, this was not a very rational act itself.'* Indeed, I could have thought of a better way to propose than being stuck at home with my fiancé, but that's beside the point. By saving money and being engaged, what 'rational me' should have probably thought was, "Ok, money is still coming in, and I have a wedding to organise, so I will be putting my additional savings into a wedding fund."

Instead, what I thought was, "I know I need to save for a wedding, but I've already put some money on the side. I have pre-allocated the rest to my planned monthly spending budget; this is money that I planned to spend anyway, I so might as well do that. This being the case, let's see what I need. One – a barbeque. So, I live in a flat, my balcony isn't that big and already pretty crowded. BUT it is getting nice and warm outside. Wouldn't it be lovely to have a barbeque? Two - cigars. I am not a smoker and have never been one, but why don't I buy a box of cigars to celebrate my engagement, only because it would be cool to flaunt some stylish cigars with my whiskey? Sounds like a plan. Three – globe-shaped whiskey decanter. There's nothing wrong with my old decanter or even keeping whiskey in the bottle, but wouldn't alcohol just look way, way better in a globe decanter!" The list goes on and on, but you get the drift. Surely, I am not the only one with a complete list of avoidable (well, useless!) stuff.

Example 2 – Toilet paper

This one has got to me my favourite – toilet paper! I think there is overwhelming consensus on the fact that toilet paper is super important. It might not hit one's top 10 list of items to pick if one were stranded on a desert island and fighting for survival, but the corona virus really highlighted the immense significance of toilet paper. I cannot be the only person thinking that what we witnessed at the beginning of the pandemic was beyond ridiculous. Who could have imagined that of all catastrophes the pandemic could inflict on our lives, toilet paper shortage would be one of them? I can still come to terms with face masks, hand sanitisers, or other medical kits shortages, but toilet paper? This really blows my mind. Let's put things into perspective. Toilet paper revenues in March 2020 were estimated to be 98% higher than March 2019 in Australia, 82% in Spain, 80% in the UK, etc[1]. A UK-based IT student even went on to publish an online toilet paper calculator. Based on over 2 million visits, users on average had 500% more toilet paper than they needed for the mandated 2-week quarantine period[2]. Irrational behaviour does not need a greater advertisement than this!

Example 3 – Savings and debt addiction

Let's now divert our attention to the savings habit of UK citizens. Logically, it makes a lot of sense to save money, be it for your child's college, period of potential unemployment, healthcare expenditures, or retirement planning. And yet, a recent survey among 2000 people in the UK suggested that around 33% of people in the UK had less than £1,500 in the bank, and 15% had no savings at all[3]. To make things worse, an estimated half of the UK consumers started 2020 with some form of personal debt, and about 5 million people owned over £10 000 in loans and credit[4]. This is no laughable matter. But while many people genuinely struggle to make ends meet, a lot of us are just addicted to buying stuff. We are a country that is (almost willingly) addicted to debt. Exotic holidays, newer cars, the latest smart phones, slimmer and better TVs... It all goes on the credit card. Of course, none of it is essential, but we happily spend money today, while planning for the future just does not seem so important. I witnessed a young lady in a jewellery shop explaining to the sales assistant how she would be back in a few days once her credit card was approved to pay for that cherished diamond ring. Maybe I just do not have my priorities right but getting a credit card to buy yourself a diamond ring, does not sound particularly rational. But I am a man. What do I know about women's love for diamonds…

Example 4 – Jealousy

Jealousy – this is another touchy topic but one of the most obvious ones. When it comes to love and human emotions, rationality invariably finds itself at the receiving end. We all know someone, or this someone could be us, who is completely obsessed with their partner and suspects every other man or woman of trying to steal them. If you have been checking your partner's ex's social media, browsing through your partner's phone while they are in the shower, or taking a peek at the glaring screen every time their phone buzzes, you know what I am talking about. And while we might be right in some cases in that they may indeed have an affair, most times, we are only self-destructive by playing out various scenarios in our heads, which bear no relation to the truth. The fact is, we carry a lot of baggage from previous relationships and experiences, and we end up projecting them on our current relationships, driving ourselves crazy in the process.

Example 5 – Judging by the cover

Last one – judgement. We would like to think that when it comes to serious matters, we can invoke every rational brain cell in our heads while keeping emotions at bay. I recently watched a TV programme called '100 Humans'[5]. It is a show, run by three young scientists who conducted a series of experiments on 100 people. In one of them, they randomly divided the participants into two groups of 50 and showed them pictures of people (actors) who had allegedly committed crimes. The difference is that while the crime scenarios remained unchanged, the pictures projected each group to be different. Group one was given pictures of people who were widely considered better looking, while the second group was given pictures of not-so-good-looking people. Each participant was asked to pass a sentence based on these pictures and a succinct narrative of the alleged crime. Theoretically, one would opine that 'criminals', who had committed the same crime, would receive a similar, if not the same, sentence. It does make logical sense for this to be the case. However, the reality was starkly different. Suprisingly, the participants were strongly influenced by physical appearances and consistently handed out less stringent punishments to better-looking 'criminals'. So much for objectivity…

I can pull a lot more examples, and surely you can too. Irrationality is rife in our lives, whether it comes to shopping habits, relationships with other people, or work. We are simply not hardwired to be these perfectly logical, rational, value-optimising human beings that traditional economic theory would have us believe. But here's the thing I want you to know and believe. This is perfectly fine. One of the main takeaways of this book is that when it comes to ourselves and others, we are who we are and should really learn to live with it. Before we move on, I want to spend a few minutes talking about the examples mentioned above and expound on the forces in play here. This is useful because it will illustrate the myriad of influences that mould our behaviour - consciously or subconsciously.

Example 1 – I don't really need this, I will buy it - Explained

I would like to look into a couple of different aspects here:

1. Mental accounting
2. Reasons for buying all of this unnecessary stuff, in general, and specifically in my case

So, the concept of mental accounting was posited by the famous American economist and behavioural scientist Richard Thaler[6], but we are all familiar with it. Simply, it means that we tend to put our expenditures in different categories, e.g., a pot of money for the rent and bills this month, another pot as saving for the big holiday you want to go to next month, a third pot for social activities, etc. I hope you get the drift. Quite often, the simplest of notions are camouflaged behind obscure names. So, this is how mental accounting works: in our heads (or if you prefer notepads and spreadsheets, whatever floats our boat), we allocate a sum of money for every main category of expenditures we have and treat them as distinct pots of money. Going back to my example, I had allocated (in my head) a pot of money for monthly expenditures and entertainment. This was completely distinct from the rent and bills pot, and it was meant to be spent all along, which explains why I had no trouble spending this money as long as I was not compromising any of the other pots. Let's consider another instance. Have you gone on a holiday with a fixed budget in mind, say £1,000, only to find out on the last day that you have not been spending as much as originally thought and you still have some money left? Now you have two options: option 1 – continue spending at your current rate and go back home with a nice saving; option 2) – "nah, this money was meant to be spent in the first place, so drinks on me tonight, boys and girls!" The same principle holds true.

Now, moving on to the second aspect – why do we end up buying all this stuff we don't really need? The list of reasons here is not an exhaustive one, but here are some of the key ones:

1. **Media influence and marketing**. If you are already thinking, "that doesn't apply to me, maybe someone else could be influenced by marketing tricks, but not me, I am smarter than this", pat yourself on the back. You're a perfectly normal average person because most of us think the same. Did you know that the average modern person is exposed to roughly 5000 ads a day? Staggering, isn't it? TV ads, signage on stores, road billboards,

ads on social media, banners popping up on your phone, everything adds up. Luckily, we don't consciously register most of them. Otherwise, we will go mental due to information overload (which is endemic in itself, but let's save that topic for another day). We do absorb them subconsciously. So, visualize this: you coincidentally crave ice cream in the evening after not really seeing the ice cream ad, and end up ordering a new T-shirt online because the other 20 T-shirts in your wardrobe aren't good enough anymore. You may want to reconsider your decision.

2. **Peer pressure.** Does your child come back home after school and asks for the latest, or at least a newer version of a popular smartphone brand because everyone at school already has it, and theirs isn't cool enough anymore? You will probably think that kids do it, but you are a grown-up, and fads do not influence you as much. You could be right, but do you remember the expensive holiday to Bali, Barbados or New Zealand, which you could not really afford but you booked anyway only because all of your friends had recently booked a nice exotic trip and you did not want to come across as the impoverished or dreary one? If you do, do not feel bad about it; it is only normal. We are, by nature, social animals, and the sense of belonging is one of our most visceral human needs. Whether this means, buying a particular brand of runners, booking a long-haul flight, or drinking on a night out due to vacuous considera-

tions or peer pressure, we try to conform to social normal a lot more than we care to admit.

3. **Discounts and promotions**. Let's go back to marketing for a moment and look at discounts, promotions, and limited-time offers. There are compelling marketing tools that leave no stone unturned in trying to convince us that we want something, and we want it now, like irredeemably rapacious creatures. Thriving on the phenomenon of instant gratification, they work similarly – creating a feeling that we will be getting a great value for money if we buy the product, and more importantly, we should do it pretty quickly, before regular prices returned. They work because we absolutely hate the thought of missing out (also known as Fear of Missing Out or FOMO in modern parlance). One could write a whole book only on this topic, but that's not my main focus.

Example 2 - Toilet paper - Explained

I am not sure anyone can explain why toilet paper suddenly became the most popular item worldwide, but I found myself confronted with a couple of plausible explanations. According to a consumer psychologist, Dr. Catherine Jansson-Boyd, when we are anxious, we try to do something practical to give us a sense of normal things and being back in control[7]. It probably works the same as our proclivity to shut ourselves down in the face of great adversity and pretend as if nothing has transpired. I can only explain this in my head as a self-preservation mechanism. Another theory I heard is that toilet paper particularly became popular because it is quite a bulky item and stocking up with it creates the impression that we are better prepared for the quarantine. These theories are probably right, at least to an extent but let's not forget the third factor – us! Even if we were not part of the initial panic buyers, the toilet paper shortages in the shops and, as always thanks to the media, made us all very aware of our own supplies and necessity. Scared by the potential of not being able to procure toilet paper when needed, more people rushed to the stores to buy some, too, thus creating a snowball effect and aggravating the situation. And let's be clear, while these explanations sound plausible after the effect, rushing to stockpile on toilet paper at the start was nothing short of irrational behaviour exacerbated by herd psychology.

Example 3 – Savings and debt addiction – Explained

Saving and debt build-up are highly (negatively) correlated. This is to say, the presence of savings would suggest less debt as savings can be used to fund expenditures and vice versa. For this example, I will focus on savings because we have already spoken enough about spending money. You cannot talk about savings and planning for retirement without mentioning *hyperbolic discounting*[8] – BIG WORDS! Fear not, behind this shiny façade is an innately simple concept – the idea that we will happily sacrifice a bigger reward in the future for a smaller reward today. Conceptually, this is the opposite of delaying gratification. Hyperbolic discounting is everywhere around us. Think about healthy eating and exercising versus gorging on junk food, not smoking versus smoking, saving for the future versus spending money now. The former in each of these pairs requires restraint and exercise of control *now* to reap greater benefits in the future, in the form of better health, extended life expectancy, or financial stability. And while it would make a lot of sense to go for this smart/rational option, most of us consistently fail at it. The benefit of a new TV, flashier car, or that yummy greasy pizza NOW is just too good to resist. The psychology of this behaviour is very intriguing. Evolutionary psychologists attribute this to evolution and survival instincts[9]. Imagine our ancestors going on a hunt for antelopes when food and shelter were the primary drivers of utmost importance for survival. Let's assume a hunter called Steve is a very good but hungry guy. So, Steve prowls through the bushes looking for his prey when he comes across a skinny, half-grown antelope. He has a choice to make: kill and eat it now or wait for it to grow a little more and kill it later for more meat. If he decides to wait, delaying gratification, he could starve to death, so no real choice to make here, really.

Back in the day, food wasn't as ubiquitous as it is today. You could be lucky and kill a big bison today to feed the tribe for a few days or go a few days without luck, so passing on food wasn't a smart option when your very survival hinged on it. Things are different nowadays, but some of our primal instincts are so deeply ineffaceable in our brains that they often drive us without consciously realising it.

There is another factor in play here – uncertainty. Reverting to the saving example, by saving money, we forego an immediate benefit for a potentially greater benefit in the future. *Potential* is the key word here. Why would you not go to nice and sunny Spain tomorrow, only to save some money for a potential future period when you might lose your job and fail to pay your bills? In other words, foregoing a certain benefit today for a potentially greater benefit tomorrow. What if you do not lose your job because you are pretty awesome at what you do, and the company has to be mad to let you go? What if you go to Spain and win the lottery, so you wouldn't need to worry about money? What if you could find a better-paying job and you could afford holidays without compromising on saving? These are very dangerous questions, which work at the back of our minds. When we combine this with our intrinsically optimistic nature, we have little chance to win.

Example 4 – Jealousy – Explained

So, you have been dating this great guy, let's call him Mark, for a couple of years. You already live together, and during this time, he has been nothing but good and honest with you. Yet, you cannot help but check his phone every other day, take a sneak peek every time he gets a message, and rummage through the list of people liking his pictures on social media, lest someone outside the friend circle you know consistently appears on the list, much to your chagrin. You know you have no reason to doubt him, but you simply cannot help yourself. You try to fight off the doubt, successfully for a day or two, but then make just one quick check for peace of mind, and things are back to normal. Invariably, you end up detesting your insecurity and wondering what the hell is wrong with you.

Like love, jealously is a largely irrational feeling, but we can try and understand where it is coming from. Unsurprisingly, it has a lot to do with our survival instincts. Let's face it; most of us are territorial animals. We have a strong sense of ownership and feel threatened when someone comes over and wants to take what is ours. Remember the last time you saw guy A punching guy B in the pub because B was talking to A's partner? It isn't very different from two elks banging their heads together to fight over a female or status within the herd. We are no different from animals in that we are driven by the same primal instincts. We put on a suit or a nice dress, and walk into the office where we work on super important matters with other superior human beings. Then at the end of the day, we go down to the pub for a couple of quick beers after work and ring our partner who works next door. He/she joins, walks to the bar for a drink, and someone else initiates a conversation with them while waiting to order. We catch a glimpse of what is going on, walk over, take a swing, and that's it, six million years of evolution go down the drain like that.

Of course, we are not all so jealous, and what's mentioned above are some exaggerated scenarios, but most of us experience milder, episodic bouts of jealousy at one time or another. Why does it impact us differently, though? Studies on the topic find a strong correlation between jealousy and low self-esteem. Jealous types are usually the ones with lower self-esteem, people who feel they wouldn't be able to keep their partners because they are not good enough, and it is only a matter of time before someone better comes over and snatches them.

Let me add another element to this – past experiences. If you are 30+ years old, you're likely to have had a couple of past relationships that you'd much rather forget. Unfortunately, starting a new relationship isn't as easy as throwing an old T-shirt in the bin and buying a new one. We all carry baggage from past relationships and experiences, like battle scars on our hearts. Let's go back to our imaginary scenario where you have been dating this awesome guy for the last couple of years. You are trying to figure out what is wrong with you for playing out all these horrible scenarios of Mark cheating on you in your head. You don't have to try very hard, because you momentarily remember how your dad cheated on your mum with the next-door neighbour Becky. You then happen to remember how your ex would often work till late... on his colleague Wendy. All of the missing pieces seem to come together. You do not have to be a genius to decipher the root cause of your self-inflicted misery. That's a great start, so well done. It should be simple from here. Just remember that Mark is not your dad or your ex. Mark is a good man. Unfortunately, not how things work. Your try to reason with yourself, but the emotional scars are just too deep.

Example 5 - Judging by the Cover – Explained

I intend to cover this section in more detail later in the book. For the moment, let's just say that our judgement is fallible. The participants in the experiment were given a brief description of the alleged crime. This is all the information they had at their disposal. For a rational person, the picture would be irrelevant, but let's not forget, we are not rational. Looks played a big role in this experiment, by getting in the way of sound judgment. What happens, in reality, is that our brains try to consider things holistically, collating all available (which is often contradictory) information to create an opinion. While there is a logical explanation for why we do that, the downside is that we are often swayed by impertinent factors. As fascinating as our brains are, they are not impervious to some intrinsic flaws, which often work against us. But more on this, later.

If you are still awake, hopefully, at this point, you will concur that we humans are not rational beings. We are strongly influenced by deeply engrained emotions and biases in our brains, past experiences, and extraneous stimuli. There are so many influences intricately intertwined together in our psyche that rational thought is a tiny little part of the whole melting pot. We are like a bus on the road, which picks up new understandings, feelings, and experiences at every stop, except that this road goes six million years back when human evolution is considered to have started. And, this is a heck of a long road to ignore. But maybe, we do not have to ignore it. We are who we are, and at the end of the day, it is this beautiful fusion of rational and irrational, black and white, yin and yang, which makes us human, imperfect, fallible but human.

5

Section 1 – It is All About the Ego

In this first section, I would like to look at what ego is, what its purpose is, and the various mechanisms that help it keep happy. I have wrapped up a few chapters under this section as they are complementary and add different nuances. This is important to understand how ego controls large parts of our world. Whether or not we understand it, ego has far-reaching implications for our relationship with ourselves and others, our attitude towards failure, and the importance of success.

6

Chapter 2 – Ego

"We cannot bear very much reality, we are biased to protect our egos against the onslaught of unwelcome truths."
- Garrett Hardin

This chapter is critical for understanding the world we live in and the intricate psychological forces which are in play in pretty much everything we do. It is foundational for the themes I would like to explore in the following chapters.

Without looking into ourselves first and what makes us tick, it is hard to understand society and how other people behave because society is constituted by people like us. Each one of us is an integral part of the whole, like one of the billions of neurons comprising our nerve system. But while we do tend to mull a lot about others, what someone did in the office, how your flat-mates reacted to the news that we were looking to move out, what that guy on the news did, etc., we hardly ever think about ourselves. We know when we are upset, happy, frustrated, or anxious, but we hardly ever try and understand *why*. And, I mean really why, not the superficial stories we conjure in our heads. These, by the way, play a very important role as well, but let's leave it for a bit later.

For the purposes of this book, I will use the common everyday definition of the word as our sense of self-esteem or self-worth. I am not interested in the Freudian definition of the ego, and unless you are one of those who've dedicated their lives to psychology, nor do you. Life is just too short to try and understand Freud.

The word ego usually has a negative connotation. We tend to use it way too often in the sense of inflated ego or egotism. This isn't surprising because we typically use the word to describe people who are too full of themselves. But that doesn't have to be the case. The ego itself is not a bad thing. In fact, it plays a very important role in our development, confidence, and even our very own existence. And this is one of the two main points I want to make in this chapter – ego itself is not a bad thing, similar to a hammer in one's hands. If you use it maliciously, it can kill a person, but it can build the roof above your head if you use it right. The second point is – we fiercely fight to make it a bad word.

Let's start by pointing out that the word "ego" is Latin for "I". This already explains a lot, doesn't it? We are very self-centred creatures, and a lot... or should I say most or maybe even all of what we do is for our own benefit, satisfaction, and interest. This isn't necessarily surprising if you think about it. Some would even argue that this is the most natural thing that any of us could do. It goes back to our predilection for self-preservation. When we are first born, long before developing any regard for others, we are the centre of our universe. We are the sun, the moon, and whatever else we would like to think we are. A baby doesn't worry about its mum wanting to get some sleep at 3 am, it wants food, and it wants it now! This means we are all born with the primal instinct to do what is necessary for our own survival. We are the only person that matters in our heads and the one who is always with us, so we've got to safeguard ourselves. It is not only later that we start developing an appreciation for the eight billion other people in this world, in addition to us.

Let's put our physical survival on the side for a little while. Luckily, most of us live in times when we do not have to fight daily for survival. Unfortunately, many people in certain regions of the world still do, but let's not go there for now. The world is not perfect, and it never will be; poverty and violence will continue to be factors in the global scene, at least for the foreseeable future. Despite this, we probably live in the best of times this world has ever seen, times when the main threat to us increasingly comes from the inside. So, I will move away from the view of ego as critical for physical survival and transcend into the more obscure world of the human psyche, our internal balance, and the role ego plays in these.

Think about our inner peace and its significance for us. We hardly ever realise it, but a lot of what we think and do aims to preserve this precious sense of inner peace. It is a function of how we perceive ourselves against others and the environment we are in. Feelings of stress, anxiety, and dissatisfaction stem from this peace being disrupted. A healthy consciousness requires us to feel good about ourselves, to feel valued and appreciated by others. Think of our inner piece as an imaginary scale, which needs to be balanced for us to feel satisfied. Ego plays an important role here, ensuring this scale remains balanced. Tip it to one side, and we get a hyperbolic view of our own self-worth. This is the ego we usually perceive when we hear the word, this grotesque, delusional conception that we know better, we are better, and we are the only thing that matters. This is what the famous author Ryan Holiday portrays in his bestseller "Ego is the Enemy"[10] refers to as the main deterrent to success (excellent book, by the way, strongly recommend it to everyone). However, just tip the scale to the other side, and you get to the other end of the spectrum where very low ego can be just as detrimental. Thinking too little of ourselves can stymie success and happiness just as much as heightened ego does. And this is the side I want to spend more time on. An inflated ego is more common; we all have a strong opinion about egotism, but we don't often think about the contrasting scenario. Negligible ego, I could argue, is just as bad if not worse. This is because, unlike the heightened ego, which displeases others, but helps us feel good about ourselves, a low ego causes internal misbalance and dissatisfaction; it hurts our inner peace and shakes the very foundation of what we hold dear to us. Let's look at a couple of examples.

Example 1 – Becky

Becky is a wonderful young woman in her early 30s. She is attractive, educated, comes from a good family, and her friends adore her. It would not be far-fetched to say that Becky is a catch. However, Becky was quite unfortunate in her previous two relationships. In her early 20s, she dated Patrick, roughly the same age but a bit of a player. He liked going out with his friends and, being young, didn't care too much about loyalty. Being perceived as cool and being a player among his friends was more important to him. So, he cheated a few times. What a douche! When Becky found out, it was over. A couple of years later, Becky fell in love again, this time with Stuart. He was a personable, well-spoken, and promising young man working as a salesman for an IT company, with a global clientele. Nothing beats a good face-to-face client meeting, sometimes followed by posh wining and dining, so Stuart travelled quite a bit for work, sometimes for extended periods. Earning well in commissions, being away from Becky for longer periods, and in places where no one knew him, Stuart didn't show much restraint either. Another douche! So, this relationship didn't quite work out well too. A few years of Becky's youth went down the drain. Now she is in her early 30s and has been with Ben for a few months. Ben is an excellent guy - educated, good-looking, well-raised, fully committed to Becky, and loving her to bits. He sees a future with her, and so does she - but something at the back of her mind makes her restless. Despite clearly realising Ben's worth, she cannot eliminate the lingering fear that he will betray her too. After all everyone else did, why would he be any different? She was still young, but she wasn't 22 anymore. She possessed many qualities, but would they be enough to keep him around or some younger and prettier girl would come and snatch him? As their relationship strengthened and she became more emotionally invested in it, the fears grew (she had more to lose now). Her confidence was so damaged from the previous relationships that she constantly feared she wouldn't be good enough to keep him. She had nightmares and panic attacks when he occasionally went out with friends or worked late in the office. The thought of him cheating when not with her led to many arguments between them. One Saturday after the third argument for the week, Ben packed up and left, and yet another relationship went down in history, leaving Becky in pieces. The difference this time is that it wasn't Ben's fault. Despite his sincere love for her, Becky's insecurities and the ensuing scandals became too much for him to hear.

Example 2 - John

John is 33. He is the youngest of three kids and lives in New York. John's elder brother Cameron is 37, and his elder sister Michelle is 35. John's childhood was far from easy. Cameron always had an aptitude for physics and showed potential for becoming an excellent physicist from an early age. Being the first born, he was the biggest pride of his parents. All these family gatherings and barbeques with friends were a real treat for him. "Cameron got the highest grade on the recent exam",

"Cameron won that award last week", "Cameron would represent the school at the state science fair next month", you wouldn't hear the end of it. Michelle, on the other side, was a talented musician. She had a real gift for playing the piano and went on to play at various gala dinners and events across the country. And then we have John. He was an intelligent kid with many interests but no particular talent for anything. Not only did he grow up in the shadow of his elder siblings, but his parents also wouldn't miss a chance to remind him he wasn't as good as Cameron and Michelle each time he would do something wrong. It was not that he was not disciplined or well-behaved. He was a good kid. Imagine growing up in a family where whatever you do is never good enough, and even worse – you get constantly reminded of it. Needless to say, John grew up very introverted, shying away from the other kids, trying to not cause much trouble, and giving people yet another reason to remind him about his perceived uselessness. Back to the present. He has been working at a local diner for the past seven years and wouldn't leave the job and look for something else, despite having the qualities to achieve a lot more. He lives in New York, after all, a city of over eight million people, why would anyone hire him instead of all those other bright sparks?

Both of these examples are fictional, but I am sure many of us can relate to them or know people who can. All I want to show is that having a low perception of your own self-worth can be a serious impediment to your happiness, progression, and success. In reality, my personal opinion is that it is actually worse than having an inflated view of your own worth, talent, or skill. Think about all successful people in this world and how they got to where they are. Barak Obama wouldn't have run for the presidency if he did not believe he had what it took to become one or wasn't better than his opponents. Jeff Bezos would not have founded Amazon, subsequently becoming the richest man on Earth, hadn't he believed that his idea was better than many other dot com start-ups in the 1990s. Tom Cruise wouldn't have become the world-renowned actor and multi-millionaire, hadn't he believed he was better than everyone else for the leading role in *Risky Business,* the 1983 comedy film, which catapulted him to new heights of stardom. The unifying thread among them is that they all believed they were not only good but the best for this new beginning (and, of course, had the qualities to back them up). It can be inferred that they did not have an inflated ego or unrealistic view of themselves and that could be totally true; I am not saying any of them is an egotist. I am trying to say that we all need this almost romantic, a little dreamish disconnect to reality to achieve greatness. Because to achieve success, you first need to be a dreamer.

Hopefully, at this point, I have managed to make the point that ego is paramount for our emotional balance and well-being. We hardly ever think of this consciously, but on a deep subconscious level, our brain works tirelessly to generate ideas, concepts, and theories to support this emotional balance. It keeps telling us that it isn't our fault, that we are better, and that we know better because we need this reinforcement to maintain a healthy relationship with ourselves, even if this may mean a skewed relationship with reality.

7

Chapter 3 - Superiority Illusion

"It is not true that people are naturally equal for no two people can be together for even a half an hour without one acquiring an evident superiority over the other."

- Samuel Jackson

Having laid the foundations of the purpose of ego in the previous chapter and highlighting its importance for our internal balance, this and the next three chapters will look into specific biases and mental shortcuts, which underpin this all-important balance by feeding our ego. Don't get me wrong, I am in love with ego, but because, as we will see later in the book, there is a lot in life, which comes down to it – interactions with others, fear of failure, how we interpret things, why we constantly compare to others, etc. Ego protection will be underscored many times in these later chapters, so I would like to explore it fully.

Let's start with Superiority Illusion (a.k.a. Illusory Superiority) and one of my favourite examples. It was the morning of 19th April 1995 in Pittsburgh. A man walked into a bank and robbed it at gunpoint without even wearing a mask. He walked out with a bag full of cash and let out a sly smile at the camera. A few hours later, he robbed another bank in the same manner. One of the coolest bank robbers in the world! Later that night, just after midnight, McArthur Wheeler was arrested in his home and left in utter disbelief how the police managed to identify him[11]. He "wore the juice" after all! What happened there is that Mr. Wheeler had rubbed lemon juice on his face because he thought that doing so would render him invisible to the cameras. Lemon juice is used in the creation of invisible ink, so rubbing some on his face would have made him invisible too. Sounds perfectly reasonable to me. Yet, Wheeler didn't go down in history as the smartest bank robber. Still, his case ignited much debate and research into the psychology of overconfidence and our proclivity to hold favourable views of our own abilities, which are closely related to superiority illusion.

Simply put, superiority illusion12 is a cognitive bias whereby an individual overestimates their own qualities and views themselves more favourably than others. The most common example, which you will recognise right away is the "I am above average at..." Seriously, the list here is virtually endless. After all, the typical man is above average at driving, fighting, and drinking. We also have above-average looks and brains. I reckon these are the standard ones, but there will be a lot more based on the person. What are you above average at?

Disclaimer: Like with many things in life, I am making various generalisations throughout this book to portray general patterns and tendencies, but there are bound to be many exceptions, so let's be mindful of this.

On the page of Superiority Illusion, it is notable that there will be marked cultural differences. Western cultures, which are intrinsically self-centred, would tend to exhibit stronger self-esteem boosting biases and tendencies than their eastern counterparts.

Right, back to Superiority Illusion. Let's look into why we exhibit it and some common examples in everyday life. This is a well-researched area of psychological behaviour, and some interesting examples of unhinged recalcitrance abound. Some of the most popular ones include:

- 65% of Americans consider their intelligence above-average[13]
- 90% of drivers rate themselves above-average in terms of skills[14]
- 94% of teachers rate themselves above-average compared to their fellows[14]

Clearly, from a statistical point of view, everyone can't be above average, so what is the problem here? Are we overly optimistic about our own skills and value? Are we bad at appreciating the qualities of others? Are we using an erroneous approach by comparing ourselves with others? I would say, all the above. It is important to look at each of these as they are paramount to understanding why we tend to think more highly of ourselves but never fail to judge others. Because we are particularly good at making excuses for ourselves while judging everyone else.

"I am not average."

Let's start with the simplest explanation – we just do not like the thought of being average. Average implies we are like everyone else! It means there is nothing special or unique about us and this simply cannot be true. My parents did NOT raise an average person. I can list plenty of cases when my mum and my grandma claimed I was special. They would never lie to me. If they say I am special, then I've got to be. Most of us are raised in warm and nurturing environments where those close to us praise us even when we do not entirely deserve it. I do remember being praised by my parents for my drawing skills when I was young. Well, those statements were blatant lies. Even today, my drawing could really give a 5-year-old kid a run for its money. Then, you have the marketers, who come over and tell us that we could customize our T-shirt, trainers, phone, car, virtually anything these days to match our UNIQUE identities. It isn't hard to grow our little bubble and believe we are the best thing this world has ever seen and will ever see. Naturally, it is hard to fathom that we are average. A note of caution: if your ex is telling you that you are like everyone else, do not listen to them. Exes are a lousy source of reference.

"It was not my fault."

We already discussed our psychological need to see ourselves favourably and its importance for our mental health. This is responsible for us having a massive blind spot for our own faults and mistakes, more like a blind Pacific Ocean. This blind spot is constantly reinforced by the various narratives, and excuses we make in our heads to explain our own mistakes, faults, and deficiencies. There are countless examples of this in our everyday lives, from the most trivial and insignificant mundane tasks to work problems or interactions with friends and family. Have you forgotten to buy something from the shop, because you had to do so much and cannot think of everything? Have you had a car accident, which was everyone else's fault, but yours? Have you failed an exam, because the teacher did not like you or asked you that one question you did not know, while you knew everything else? Have you missed a deadline at work, not because you couldn't manage your workload properly, but because you were the only one doing work and you could not do everything? I bet the answer to at least a few of these is "Yes!" While some of these could be perfectly valid explanations i.e., that car accident genuinely was not your fault, we often distort the truth. It is truly amazing to see how creative we can be in making excuses. I remember a person close to me lost their phone a few years back. I choose to protect this person's identity and instead of mum, I will call them Mrs. D. So, Mrs. D lost her phone... for the third time. However, it wasn't Mrs. D's fault, it was her husband's – Mr. D's. This is what happened. Mr. D called Mrs. D on her mobile. After the call, Mrs. D would attempt to drop the phone back in her coat's pocket, but unfortunately, the phone had slipped and fallen on the ground, never to be seen again. The explanation here is simple – if Mr. D hadn't called, Mrs. D would have never taken the phone out of the pocket in the first place, and it wouldn't have gone missing. Makes sense, doesn't it? You got to love the lengths to which people go to justify things in their heads.

I am trying to say that we always have an excuse for what we or people close to us have done. But how about everyone else? How often do we step into other peoples' shoes and try to justify their actions? In my experience – not too often, or at least not as often as we do for ourselves. Person A should have been looking at the road when making that turn. Person B should have studied harder for the exam. Person C should have been keeping closer attention to their book of work. Mrs. D should have been more careful returning the phone to her pocket. As you can see, it is easy to see how we can be left with the impression that our faults are not *really our faults*, whereas everyone else's faults are their faults. All this perpetuates the sweet illusion that we are better than the rest. Hence, it is hardly a surprise that many of us think of ourselves as above average.

Lack of information

Lack of information is another common reason for the superiority illusion. Similar to the point above, it is premised on the fact that we hardly ever try to put ourselves in someone else's shoes, and very often, we can't even do it. Very often, we use mental shortcuts to make conclusions about everything and everyone around us. We form opinions based on what we see, which in most cases, is limited and only a fraction of the complete picture. While there is a perfectly good reason for this, it often works against us, as conclusions made on partial information tend to be both wrong and egregious. To be clear, when I say partial, as opposed to complete information, I am not talking about perfect information here. Perfect information is just a non-existent theoretical concept. I use complete information in the sense of having as many details we can access as possible. Let me give you an example. So, let's say you are working on a project in the office and come across a specific problem. Your colleague A, from another team, owns the issue resolution. He suggests that there could be a couple of ways to fix this, but the best approach is Y. You are not that close to the issue but have some knowledge in the area. So based on what you know, Y doesn't sound ideal. In your view, solution Z would be a lot more elegant. This isn't your problem, or even your team's problem, so you don't really care. You have your own problems to deal with anyway, but you are left with the impression that colleague A might not be particularly good at what they do…not as good as you are anyway. Of course, what you do not see here is the rest of the picture. You have concluded that your solution is better than theirs based on what you know, but you expose yourself to the possibility of being completely oblivious to all other details, which could render your solution impractical or even unfeasible. All you know is that you are more intelligent than colleague Y. Now, repeat this a few more times with colleagues B, C, D, etc., and you are already the smartest person in the office, or at least well above average.

Lack of honest feedback

We all need a reality check from time to time. The above points have demonstrated how we could end up with a distorted view of reality when it comes to our knowledge, traits, and abilities in relation to others. So, receiving honest feedback is important to keep our feet on the ground. The problem is, this is difficult to come across, whether at work or in personal life. There are a couple of factors in play here: 1 - we absolutely hate being criticised, 2 - we are a lot better at praising than criticizing, whether because we tend to avoid conflict or because we do not want to hurt someone's feelings.

Some of us are better at receiving criticism than others. I must admit, I am not "some of us". But while there are variations, generally, nobody likes being criticised. We all could possibly agree on the fact that honesty is a virtue. We could also agree that having reality checks is also a sensible thing to do from time to time. But, God, do we hate criticism! Honesty (including honest negative feedback) is one thing that sounds great in theory, and we say we want it, but we do not. We only like honesty when it inflates our bubble, not when it bursts it. And adding "constructive" to it makes no difference at all. If you do not believe me, just try and tell your partner they have put on a bit of weight, and those skinny jeans do not fit as well anymore, so maybe they are better off putting on something else. If you do so, please give me a video call and 5 minutes' notice to get the popcorn.

Have you ever wondered why your friends are exactly those certain individuals and not others? Common interests, common upbringing, being understanding and supportive of one another? All of these make sense, but have you thought that maybe it is also because they make you feel good by not criticising you very often? Would they be your friends if they regularly highlighted your flaws? Most probably not because why would you have unsupportive, insensitive, difficult friends in the first place? The truth is, they might just be honest and not afraid to call out your flaws, but in your mind, *they are just being insensitive, they want to shoot you down, they are jealous of you...* two sides of the same coin. Hence, we end up with friends who make us feel good, praise us, bring us up, exactly how we like it.

It is not only receiving honest feedback that matters; it is also to give it. I love praising my friends and colleagues. They get a nice warm feeling, and so I do; everyone is happy. But how about negative feedback? If you are anything like me, you would hate it. I need to repeat a speech five times in my head before delivering negative feedback, trying to soften the message, a bit more every time. Yes, feedback is important, and negative feedback is even more important than a positive one, as it allows us to identify and learn from our weaknesses. Yet, it isn't nice to hear it and just as bad to deliver it. Most people generally dislike confrontation and hurting other's feelings. That's why these conversations are always awkward, and we tend to avoid them when we can.

Lack of consistent approach to measure

Last one, I promise. How do we know that we are above average? How do we measure this? In some cases, it is easy. You had C on the Math test, I had A. That one test might not be enough to conclude I am better than you at Math, but let's assume it is a reliable way of measuring our Math aptitude. If C was an average result on this test, then I am clearly above average. I can cover 100 m in 13 seconds while you take 15, so I am faster than you. We have a reliable measure for comparison in these two cases, which makes things a bit easier, but this often isn't the case. Let's look at the following examples. Am I above average popular at school? Am I above-average smart? Am I above average successful? How do we measure these?

- Am I above average popular at school because I would stay late at the bar and drink when most of my classmates would have gone home by this time, so I am considered cool? Because I dated more girls/boys than my

fellow classmates? Because I smoked weed and hanged out with the cool kids? How do we measure popularity?
- Am I above-average smart because I had higher grades at school or university? Because I got a good job? Because I can do calculus in my head or speak a few languages? How do we even define smart?
- Am I above average successful because I earn more than my peers around the same age? Because I have a better family? Because I have done this or that? Because I have a Gucci bag?

Usually, we do not have fixed criteria to measure these things because they are abstract, almost subliminal, in many ways. Everyone interprets intelligence, popularity, and success differently and, by extension, classify people differently based on their prejudiced criteria. This exemplifies the real problem with such comparisons – we tend to pick criteria, which best serve our purpose. When we define the rules of the game, we will always be the winner.

All the above aims to show that most of us suffer from superiority illusion, albeit to varying degrees. We do not have to be an egotist to exhibit it, as egotism is an extreme form. Most of us would exhibit milder effects but do, nonetheless. Our sanity needs to have a bit of an inflated view of ourselves, and it is also perfectly natural. We need to believe we are good, knowledgeable, capable, deserving. Our brains have realised this a long time ago and make excellent use of our environment and externalities to perpetuate these perceptions.

Or should I say illusions? Unwillingness to admit we are just like everyone else, blame-shifting, narrative creation, moulding our environment or criteria to fit our purposes are only part of the strategies we consciously and subconsciously employ to this same end. This is what helps us not only get through the day but also aspire and reach for more.

8

Chapter 4 – Cognitive Dissonance Reduction

"He had very few doubts, and when the facts contradicted his views on life, he shut his eyes in disapproval."
— Hermann Hesse

In the 1950s, a Chicago housewife Dorothy Martin persuaded a group of people that she could communicate with aliens, and they had alerted her of a flood, which would allegedly destroy the Earth on 21st Dec 1954. However, they had nothing to worry about because those friendly aliens would come just before the flood and save her and all true believers. All they needed to do was to believe. Many of her followers left their spouses, sold their properties, and spent their money preparing for their alien rescue. The cult gathered on a fateful night, awaiting the alien arrival. But, surprise...surprise...no aliens appeared! There was no flood either.

The outcome of this story might surprise many. While some followers regretted wasting time, money, and effort after coming to their senses, many fervent believers even strengthened their beliefs, contending that the calamity had only been averted by their actions and commitment. They believed that God had decided to spare the Earth and cancel the flooding due to their commitment to the cause, and the light spread by their actions[15].

Similarly, Barack Obama's candidacy for US president spurred heated debates around his eligibility. As many as 25% of the US adults believed Obama's candidacy was unlawful because he was allegedly not a natural-born US citizen, which was a constitutional requirement. The so-called 'birthers' believed he was born in Kenya, making him ineligible to run for a US president[16]. In 2010, Obama published his Hawaiian birth certificate. Similar to the alien cult, this convinced some of the 'birthers' that he was legitimate, but various conspiracy theories were peddled by hard believers claiming that the document was fabricated. This only strengthened their conviction that they were right if he had gone through that effort to fabricate the document. And, why did it take two years to publish? Clearly, something was wrong.

It is curious that in both examples, hard believers refuted the proof and strengthened their convictions when presented with proof. The psychology behind it is interesting, and it is one of my favourite psychological concepts. In reality, it is quite simple, and we do encounter it all the time, possibly without realizing it. In popular psychological parlance, it is known as cognitive dissonance reduction. Most simply put, the theory posits that holding conflicting views or attitudes, or experiencing events, which conflict with our pre-held beliefs causes a psychological tension in our heads. This is a feeling of unease caused by these conflicting beliefs and/or experiences. This is the part that is specific to cognitive dissonance. To ensure our mental health and inner peace, it is important to maintain consistency of beliefs and actions. This is not unlike the warm feeling we get when others agree with us and getting all edgy or upset when they don't. When this happens, our brains detect the inconsistency and try to reduce it (the reduction part). This can be done in a number of ways. Leon Festinger was the first one to observe this by studying the alien cult I mentioned at the start of the chapter[17]. If this is confusing, here are a couple of simple, everyday examples to illustrate the point.

Example 1:

Background: Anne has a decent stable job and comfortable life. But she gets an offer to temporarily move to South Africa and work there for a while, earning more money. Not being a very adventurous person by nature, she is sceptical about the offer. It cannot possibly be true! It is a small company, fairly recently established without a long and proven track record, but potentially excellent growth opportunities. However, she feels like she would not want to miss out.

She accepts the new job, packs up, and leaves. In three months, however, the local company goes bust. She only gets part of her promised salary for the period and needs to return to her home country and seek another job.

Belief: *Anne is smart and carefully assesses the pros and cons of taking the job. She would not make hasty decisions or do something stupid. It could be too good to be true, but equally, it might just be a rare opportunity.*

Reality: *Anne lost a lot of money in unpaid salary and unemployment (between return to her home country and finding a new job there), and a rift has been created between her and her partner; the whole thing was a total disaster. What a schmuck!*

Cognitive dissonance: *Anne is smart and rational, but clearly did not see that coming. Maybe she is not that smart after all. Argh...*

Example 2:

Belief: *Tom is an environmentalist. He cares about the environment a lot and is worried about gas emissions being detrimental to it. Planes are especially bad!*

Action: *Tom earns well and catches a plane to go on a holiday a few times a year.*

Cognitive dissonance: *Tom cares about the environment but still flies on a plane for leisure instead of staying local, thus causing environmental damage.*

We can find plenty more examples in everyday life, e.g., keeping fit, smoking, shopping, cheating, pretty much everything. Now, we are left with this disenchanting dis-harmony, courtesy dissonance (cognitive or otherwise, pun intended), which makes us feel uneasy. Sometimes the unease could be pretty mild, and we do not consciously register it. At other times, it could be more severe and keep us up at night.

When we discussed ego in the earlier chapters, I mentioned the importance of psychological equilibrium for our sanity and wellbeing. Our beliefs and actions need to be congruent to support the equilibrium. When this is not the case, like with the cult and birthers examples, the equilibrium is disturbed we end up feeling restless. But our brains are unique organs. They sense the imbalance and take action to remedy the situation. This is where the "reduction" part comes in. Expanding on our earlier examples would help to illustrate this.

Anne

Anne is feeling uneasy about the whole experience she had. Leaving her stable job and relocating to the other side of the world, only for things to go south shortly after, wasn't her smartest move. Perhaps, she isn't so smart or calculated as she would like to think. So, she tries to draw some conclusions and re-evaluate the situation. Yes, it had serious financial implications, and she lost money. However, was it all so bad? Probably not. He got the opportunity to travel around a bit, which was a welcome respite as he had never been to that part of the world. The weather was a lot better in South Africa than in Europe and had a nice, chilled vibe. She expanded her professional network a little bit and learning something from her mistake. So overall, it wasn't that bad, was it? Maybe she isn't stupid after all because the experience wasn't a total disaster, just a small setback, which had its positives as well. And who doesn't have one of these every now and again?

Tom

Tom feels a slight unease by flying for holidays, even though this is detrimental to the environment, which he does care about. But in the end, is his footprint so significant? He is thinking this through. Those flights will happen with or without him on board, so he isn't really making things worse. Besides, he is flying with low emission aircraft, which are more environmentally friendly than others. And finally, he does a lot of other voluntary work to help the environment, which surely must compensate for his occasional flight.

Does either of these sound like a story you have told yourself recently? The cognitive dissonance theory suggests that when we have two conflicting beliefs or actions, we will try to reduce the impact of one of them to re-establish our sense of internal harmony. This is exactly what was observed with the UFO cult followers too. When confronted with a fact – no UFOs and no calamities, which would conflict with their logically incoherent beliefs, they came up with an alternative explanation – their commitment to the cause rescued the world. I would like to say this could be a credible explanation, but that might not be the right way to describe it. Otherwise, they would face the lot harder truth to swallow – *"we were very mis-*

taken", to put this courteously. They wouldn't agree that their views may have bordered on the risible.

I am writing about cognitive dissonance reduction because, like illusory superiority, it is a cognitive mechanism for preserving our inner balance, for reassuring us that we are not all that bad, that we have not done anything wrong, or at least not that wrong. It allows us to preserve this positive view of ourselves that is beyond vital for our well-being. We do not necessarily experience the same effects when evaluating others' actions and decisions, which only contributes to our delusion of superiority and makes it much easier to judge others. It acts as a veneer of sorts that hides our flaws while exposing everyone else's. Hence, we are sometimes prone to criticising others and making them look inferior to us in comparison. But that is normal because, at the end of the day, we are not made to be perfect; we are made to be human.

9

Chapter 5 – Self-Handicapping

"The reason that I can't find the enemy is that I have yet to look within myself."
— Craig D. Lounsbrough

In the previous three chapters, we discussed the ego's purpose along with some rudimentary beliefs and cognitive strategies aimed at protecting it. All of this is for the sole purpose of maintaining a positive image of ourselves. But what if I tell you that we are equally vulnerable to self-sabotage? Sounds ridiculous, doesn't it? Why on Earth would I sabotage myself? Surely, if there is one thing that this book has made clear so far is that we do a lot to protect ourselves, consciously and subconsciously, so self-sabotage would contradict everything said so far, let alone being totally illogical. Well, not necessarily. Sabotaging our life or future, and sabotaging our ego are quite different things, as we shall uncover. As a matter of fact, the latter doesn't care one bit about the former. It would do anything to stay safe, even if this means ruining everything else around it.

In the late 1970s, two scholars, Edward Jones and Steven Berglas, observed this psychological phenomenon, which continues to be the subject of plenty of research. They called it self-handicapping[18]. Self-handicapping is a cognitive strategy whereby one would create hurdles on the road to success when facing the possibility of failure to protect their ego. Allow me to elaborate. Our ego is addicted to *being right* and *succeeding*. This is what feeds it. Every "I told you so", every small win, however insignificant, every little sense of triumphalism, boosts our self-perception of being better, smarter, and stronger. On the other hand, failure inflicts damage upon this perception. Failure is the bad guy, and we try to avoid it. Doesn't failure mean we are not so good, capable, or deserving as we would like to think we are? A smart person could think that failure is actually a good thing, that we learn from it, that it makes us stronger, and that success can only be achieved via failure. These would be perfectly rational thoughts if we take a long-term view and see failure as a stepping stone and a learning opportunity. Unfortunately, ego is primal and takes everything at face value. It does not distinguish between short-term pain and long-term gain. This implies that success means good, failure means bad. It wants more of the former and none of the latter.

Regardless of what our ego does or does not like, we live in a world when failure is an inextricable part of our lives. One cannot exist without the other: Yin and Yang, good and bad, success and failure. So, what do we do when things go wrong? We already covered some of the usual reactions in the previous chapters. We blame the failure on someone or something else, make excuses, and create narratives in our heads that are consistent with our perception that we are right and good. Self-handicapping is not much different than this. In fact, finding an excuse is the main motivation behind this cognitive strategy. The key difference here is that self-handicapping is proactive, rather than reactive. It actively seeks an excuse so that the ego is prepared when failure beckons. Most scholars distinguish two main types of handicaps: behavioural and claimed[19]. A behavioural handicap occurs when we take action to put a hurdle in our way. The most often cited example is a student going out the night before an exam. Have you done it? I have. This works in one of two ways:

1. You pass the exam or get the grade you wanted – wow, aren't you a smart one? You are so smart that you went out the night before, even got a little tipsy, but still aced that exam. They should probably name the next building on campus after you!
2. You fail the exam or do not get the desired grade – oh well, if only it hadn't been for the drinking the previous

night. You could have totally aced the exam if you had slept more and weren't feeling so rough.

In the first instance, we get an ego boost – we succeeded despite the hurdle. In the second, we have an excuse – we could have succeeded if it weren't for the alcohol. Regardless, our self-esteem is protected, and our ego is happy. Often, we do not even need to do anything to engage in self-handicapping, because inaction is also a choice. Think about a situation when you could have applied for a better role, a promotion, some programme, which could have benefited you, but you didn't. You came up with an excuse why you didn't do it – wasn't ready, the whole thing was rigged, it wasn't really worth it, etc. In many cases, these excuses camouflage the actual reason – we feared failure or rejection. Consequently, we skip a good opportunity to protect our egos from the possibility of failing and being hurt. Isn't the lack of action really an example of handicapping in this case?

The second type of self-handicap is claimed. This is where it can be inferred that there is a certain hurdle or impairment, which could stifle their performance. For example, a boxer who goes ahead with a fight, but claims he was still recovering from a previous injury or was fraught with some other predicament. The rationale behind this is the same – blaming a potential loss to the injury while taking extra credit in case of a win. We often resort to self-handicapping, because it is conducive for one of our main propensities as humans – to blame failure on external factors (externalise failure) but take credit for successes (internalise success). This is such a typical behaviour. When things go well, everyone tries to take some credit, but it is always someone else's fault when things go bad. I would be the first person to raise my hand and admit I have done that too. There is no honour in it, but we would be in heaven if we were saints, I guess.

Of course, not all of us self-handicap; some people are more likely to do it than others. Some factors that trigger this unwelcome behaviour are our self-esteem, social pressure, and expectations of those around us. The higher we climb, the harder we fall or put differently, the bigger one's ego, the worse the impact when they fail. People with higher self-esteem have more to lose, which is why they are more likely to engage in self-enhancing tactics. Likewise, fear of failure can be an important factor, too[20]. Such people can leave no stone unturned to avoid the feeling of it. This is the major paradox with self-handicapping. The more scared we are of failure, the more likely we are to induce it because it is not the failure itself that we hate but its feeling. It hurts our ego and scars our mind. The feeling we have failed is worse than the consequences of failure in our heads. Thirdly, being in the spotlight or having other people look at us could also push us towards self-handicapping. This is because, it is not just us, who we have to convince we are good, smart, or capable. We need to prove ourselves to other people as well. This is where shame enters the scene. Sometimes, doing something wrong is fine if only we know about it, but all hell breaks loose when others find out! Examples of such behaviour are in abundance: an athlete competing in a big competition when the whole world is watching; children feeling eager not to disappoint their overly ambitious parents; a video game player consciously picking a harder weapon, hero, or car to control so that doing badly could be ascribed to the choice of that object and not their skill, etc.

I know a lot of this probably does not make too much sense at face value. It is counter-intuitive, irrational, and paradoxical. And it is. A rational being would strive to maximise its chances, potential, and return. But this behaviour is not the result of a rational thought process. Going back to the first chapter, there are many situations when our monkey brains take control and make us do strange things. We are simply not as rational as we would like to think.

Self-handicapping becomes particularly problematic when it begins to impede our long-term success. It protects our self-esteem in the short term, but failure is not devoid of consequences, and we can only do it so much before it drags us to the bottom. Because after all, failure is only beneficial when we learn something from it, which is exactly what our ego inhibits. So long as it keeps telling us that it wasn't our fault, there is little motivation to improve and learn from failure. Yet, there are times when we do self-handicap, because our primal instincts do not understand the meaning of "long term", "smart", or "strategic". For them, it is all about perception. It is about protecting us from that perception of failure, which would make us look weak, undeserving, and inferior.

10

Section 2 – Brain and Heuristics

So far, this book has mainly focused on our egos and the various biases/mechanisms at play to keep them happy. This is, of course, intentional as I opine that this is the driving force behind a large aspect of our behaviour. The ego is extremely emotional, naïve, and stubborn. It is like a young child, kicking and screaming until it gets what it wants. Trying to reason with it will be just as hard as reasoning with a wall… or convincing Trump the 2020 elections were not fraudulent. Stop the count!

We will turn our attention to cognition for the next few chapters and delve deeper into how our brains work. Hang on for a second. Don't get your hopes up; they are no better. Or maybe they are, but they tend to listen to our emotions way too often. They are like puppets in the emotional theatrical show, subservient to our feelings. In the cognitive dissonance reduction chapter earlier, we already saw how our brains will often side with ego and our emotional side in an uneven battle we can hardly ever win, all the while convincing us that everything is going fine. I can only compare this twisted, yet somehow symbiotic behaviour as us being a patient, suffering from a serious disease (our overinflated ego) while the doctor (our brain) keeps lying to us that we will be fine and that there is nothing to worry about.

But, anyway, let's keep nihilism at bay for now and move on. I will use the next few chapters to look into our cognitive processes, how we make sense of the world around us, and draw conclusions. Each of these chapters will add a piece of the puzzle, just like the brain does to create an arguably plausible conclusion.

11

Chapter 6 - Cognition and Jumping to Conclusions

"Life is the art of drawing sufficient conclusions from insufficient premises."
- Samuel Butler

Humans often like to think of themselves as the masters of the world, the species on top of the food chain. In many ways, for better or for worse, this is true. We have conquered the land, the depths of the ocean, the sky, and most recently, the closer outer space (I say closer as we clearly don't know a LOT about this universe). We have control over our own lives, a lot of the processes and activities on the Earth, as well as our planet's renewable and non-renewable resources. Yes, we have indeed come to dominate the planet like no other species has before. However, we are more similar to the animal kingdom than many of us would like to admit in many ways.

Despite all our advancements in virtually every aspect of life and our firm belief in our superiority, we are, at our core, animals, driven by primal instincts to procure food and shelter, ensure security, and assert our status and dominance. This is what it comes down to. Do you get hangry (angry or irritable when hungry), and everything else starts mattering again only once you have eaten? Do you freeze or flee in the face of danger, driven by your fight or flight response? Do you want to take a swing at the guy talking to your girlfriend to assert your dominance, just like elks charging and banging their heads together over a female? Do you want to get on top of every hot guy/girl you see (this is possibly more relevant for men)? Do you remember how human you were the last time you crawled out of a club at four in the morning? We are often subservient to our primal instincts. However, that does not suggest that our instinct must be acted upon. We do possess the high intellect and sufficient willpower to often make sound and rational decisions, but our instincts and feelings influence us very frequently, whether we realise it or not.

But if one thing really distinguishes us from animals, it is our consciousness, the visceral need to know and understand the big WHY. Have you ever seen a cow grazing on some nice green grass, while thinking to itself: *Why was I born? Did God send me here for some mystical reason? If so, what would that be? Perhaps he/she wants me to eat all this grass, then produce some nice organic milk to feed the farmer and his family? Oh, such lovely grass it is! Or maybe, God didn't have a grand plan, and I decide what I want to do with my life. That's an interesting thought. Let's see...I am bored of this "job", I stand here eating grass all day and don't even get thanks in return, let alone some salary. Yeah, a salary would be nice. With that, I could go and have my hoofs polished or get a trim. You know what, that's it. I am done. If they do not appreciate me, I will quit this job and go travel the world...or check out the grass over the other side of the hill.* Even if you saw the cow, you wouldn't technically know if it thought that, but you get the drift; someone would have figured that cows could reflect on their lives.

In contrast, humans do think and ruminate on all of these things. Ever since the dawn of civilization, humans have been striving hard to unlock the secrets of the universe. *What is my place in the universe? What should my purpose in life be? Should I spend my life in humble existence and obedience, or should I give freedom to all my desires and possibly disregard all social norms, because there might be no tomorrow?* We don't often delve into such existential questions, but that does not make our quest for knowledge and finding our place in the universe any less significant. We are born curious for knowledge. We have an inborn need to know and understand. This is just how our brains are wired.

Our brains are amazing organs. They work tirelessly, day after day, year after year, from the moment they are formed to the moment we die. They constantly record and process information, looking for reasons and explanations, trying to satisfy our innate need to understand the world around us. At most times, this is a subconscious process. Sometimes, we consciously make time to reflect on our actions, the actions of others, and various events that have taken place. More often than not, we don't. But that doesn't mean there isn't a thought process going on behind closed doors. Our brains are programmed to build logical bridges between events and draw conclusions based on these experiences and observations. These conclusions are not insignificant because they help us understand if something is good or bad, safe or dangerous, desirable or undesirable. It is all part of the neverending learning process called life. Peter offended me. Hence Peter is a bad person, and we must stay away from him. Natasha, on the other hand, gave me some cake, so she is a lovely person. I like Natasha. This cognitive process is not much different today than it was thousands of years ago. We observe the environment and build logical connections to draw conclusions like our ancestors did back during Stone Age. Like Barnie five moons ago, Ken the caveman got mauled by a tiger down by the river. Hence, tigers are dangerous, and there seem to be lots of them by the river – avoid both!

Ultimately, it all comes down to survival instincts. Most of us do not have to hunt wild animals to eat and survive these days (thank God for that), but the principles remain the same at the core. Self-preservation is fundamental to our existence, and our brains understand this all too well. Whether we are talking about physical survival or preservation of our feelings and sanity, the protective function of the brain has stayed unchanged – observe and gather data, analyse these data, and draw a conclusion. Here is an important fun fact for those who are unversed with the nuances of how our brains work. We all have supercomputers in our heads, which gather and process information perpetually, even when we sleep. Everything that feels/sounds good and nice is permissible, whereas everything that makes us feel angry, upset, or worried is bad is skipped like a YouTube ad. This is how we learn and form attitudes. We form beliefs that are consistent with our experiences and attitudes. This is fundamental to our inner balance. When discussing cognitive dissonance reduction in the previous chapters, we saw how important this congruence is.

However, things in life are hardly black and white. We constantly battle with insufficient or conflicting data. The world has grown way too complex for our brains to cope with everything that life throws at us. So, what transpires when we do not have enough data to draw a reliable conclusion? The answer is, nothing changes. There isn't a big warning sign flashing on a computer screen in our head saying, "Not enough data to calculate a reliable outcome, you are in danger of drawing the wrong conclusion." Our computer will do its best to fulfil its mission, which makes it so fascinating, even if dangerous.

This might all sound confusing, but let's look at a simple example, which I hope will help imbue some clarity. Let's see how a regular computer would tackle simple math questions, compared to our brain.

Regular Computer

Problem: $2 + X = ?$

Thinking process: Hmm, I don't know X. Without X, I cannot solve this problem. I need to inform the user. He/she must give me more information.

Solution: Not enough data to solve the problem. Input X.

Brain Computer

Problem: $2 + X = ?$

Thinking process: Right, I don't know X...but, let's see what data we have in store. Searching, searching...interesting, I found references for $2 + 2 = 4$. Humans often use this example to refer to something being simple. As an expression, it is used regularly. I have found a few references when this was used. I also saw it on that ad in the underground the other day. Based on this, I can conclude that X must be 2, and the solution equals 4.

Solution: Ok, user, the answer here is 4.

This is a simplified example of how our brains are often programmed to think to make sense of the world. They are not very good at dealing with ambiguity and complexity, so shortcuts (heuristics) are in place, which endeavour to simplify this process. Most of us come up with narratives to explain certain events, but these narratives could be misleading and even dangerous as they are not always based on sound reasoning or known facts. Yet, we seem to have a lot of faith in our own logic and reasoning, often oblivious to these glaring shortcomings. This is what makes narratives powerful but often dangerous. Consider the following fictional, yet possible scenario.

Background to consider: Pete recently got married to Tina. Pete used to have a drinking problem after the demise of his parents in a tragic accident. The pain was truly overwhelming, and he could only find consolation in alcohol. He hasn't been drinking for two years now, but he has been under immense stress lately, working on a super important project with the deadline closing in on him. He was sent on a work trip to the company's head office for a week during this final stage, where he stays in a hotel.

Pete: It is 10 pm already, but Pete is still working very hard in the office. His phone is on silent somewhere under a pile of documents. Completely absorbed in his work, Pete lost track of time and forgot to give Tina a heads up that he would be working late.

Tina: Tina has been calling Pete to check up on him for the last two hours but not getting a response.

Tina's brain: Pete isn't answering the phone. He could be doing a variety of things now. Working, cheating, drinking, having had an accident on the way home, or he could even be dead... Oh, hold on - drinking! Of course he is drinking; he has been under a lot of stress. The last time this happened, he had a massive drinking problem. And, he isn't picking up the phone because he doesn't want Tina to know and have a go at him. It is clear as daylight. I must tell Tina immediately. Tinaaaaa.

Outcome of the evening when Pete finally picks up the phone: You don't even want to know...

You can see in this example how we could create various narratives in our heads to explain our surroundings and generally make sense of the world. They are very loyal but, unfortunately, prone to making premature conclusions. In many cases, these could be wrong conclusions, especially, when influenced by our emotions.

One thing that is important to consider is the direction in which our minds go. Why would Tina think Pete was drinking? Why did she not think he was gambling, cheating, or maybe had died by suicide? Of course, there could have also been more plausible explanations, like he didn't hear his phone ringing or had misplaced it. The answer is, we tend to jump to conclusions, which support our pre-existing beliefs. Since Pete has had a drinking problem, it was natural for her brain to conjure up possibilities in that direction. But it isn't just others' history and personal circumstances that impact our conclusions; it is also our own experiences, beliefs, and attitudes that matter a lot. This is what makes people interpret the same situation or scenario differently. What if Tina's father used to gamble and Tina was raised in a family where her dad would systematically come home late, regularly gambled away his salary, and always owed other people money? Her interpretation of this situation could have been completely different.

We tend to think of our emotional side as being irrational, prone to hasty decisions, and biased, whereas our brains are rational, impartial, and smart. While this simplification is a good starting point, we cannot think of one in isolation from the other. They are an indelible part of our human nature and constantly influencing one another. Attributing a wrong conclusion to a fault on the part of our supercomputer isn't right. Its function is to keep driving while our emotions shout directions on which path to take.

While we cannot always help but believe these narratives, we need to be aware of them and try to challenge them from time to time. The complexity here stems from the fact that we are not always aware of the truth. We can choose to believe one thing or another, but we might never know for sure if we are right. Who knows, maybe Pete really was drinking that night…

12

Chapter 7 - Narratives and Conclusions on Steroids

"Narrative imagining – story – is the fundamental instrument of thought. Rational capacities depend upon it. It is our chief means of looking into the future, or predicting, of planning, and of explaining."
- Mark Turner

The human brain's drive to know and to make sense of things is relentless. It is a complex organisation of billions of interconnected neurons, which tirelessly process every bit of available information that can benefit us somehow. Needless to say, this serves as a great purpose. Who wouldn't like such a powerful tool at their disposal?

These loyal neurons, however, sometimes tend to take their work too seriously. They would process away, trying to find meaning in random things and events, even where there is none. One of the characteristics of our brains and us, as humans, is that we seem to be at odds with ambiguity and complexity. We prefer single and straightforward explanations. This is why we believe in narratives and use various techniques to systemise and simplify data to more easily draw a conclusion. This is one of our natural limitations, and we would rather take a simpler (and possibly not so reliable) explanation than more complex or conflicting data, which would make it difficult for us to draw conclusions. This predisposes us to believe all kinds of stuff, as long as it provides some sort of explanation. Superstitions are a great example.

I bet you have heard some of the following superstitions:

- a broken mirror brings bad luck for seven years
- a black cat crossing your path is also bad luck (although the opposite is believed in some countries)
- finding a four-leaf clover brings good luck
- being pooped on by a bird brings riches
- touching wood brings good luck

There are thousands and thousands of such superstitions across the world. The ones listed above are widely popular, but if you add the other ones as well, which are more local and pertain to a specific country or even a region, one life will not be enough to study them all.

Superstitions are a perfect example of one's attempt to understand the world, and by extension, to influence one's good or bad fortune. How could possibly breaking a mirror bring one bad luck... other than having to clean the mess? There is no correlation between breaking a mirror and things that could be considered bad luck, like getting your car stolen, losing your purse, being fired at work, a close friend or relative falling sick, etc. Yet, ancient Romans believed that because mirrors were a reflection of the soul, breaking a mirror would, as a consequence, imply breaking one's soul. The latter would then be unable to safeguard the person from harm, hence the bad luck.

Similarly, in medieval times, black fur animals, including cats, ravens, and crows, symbolized death. This superstition has modified slightly through the centuries. Black cats are no longer harbingers of death but are still associated with bad luck.

We all know that most of these superstitions date back to ancient times. Whether their origin can be traced back to religion or national folklore, they come from dark and uneducated times, when people knew a tiny fraction of what we know today. Back then, science was studied by few and there was no Google to answer all our questions. The world had to be explained by whatever means available – spirits, gods, witches, good, or bad omens. Oh, we are indeed privileged to live in the 21st century!

But, this is not a chapter about superstitions or what qualifies as logical belief. Everyone is arguably free to believe in what they want these days, so no judging here. My only point is that superstitions are nothing else, but an alternative explanation to satiate your innate curiosity. All this goes to show is the lengths to which our minds would go searching for answers.

When I think of secret meanings, symbols, patterns, superstitions, etc., I cannot help but remember the episode of the American sitcom 'The Big Bang Theory', where Leonard and Penny give a wedding present to Sheldon and Amy. It is a brilliant example of the point I am trying to make. If you are one of those people who have the likes of "Big Bang Theory", "Friends" or "How I Met Your Mother" always in the background when doing whatever else at home, you're likely to know I am talking about. But for the benefit of those who don't quite 'get it', here's a summary.

So, Amy and Sheldon are two slightly weird scientists (in Sheldon's case, this is the understatement of the year), who got married recently. Their best friends, an already married couple, Penny and Lenard, gave them a wedding present that resembled a glass wand. The funny part in this episode is that no one actually knew the purpose of that wand. Not even Penny and Lenard, who just wanted to play a joke and enjoy Amy and Sheldon's misery, scratching their heads in search of its meaning and purpose.

Amy and Sheldon hypothesize this is a clue for a scavenger hunt they are meant to go on to discover the real purpose of the present. This leads them to the coffee shop where they first met. They decide to look into the lost and found box because they were (arguably) lost before they found each other. They find a locket in the box and are eager to see what's inside, but it turns out to be empty when they do. But this, of course, made perfect sense to them because they just got married and their journey together just started, so they will be filling it up with memories together. They also find a pair of sunglasses, making sense because they look forward to a bright future together. And all of that, based on a crystal object. Imagine what the human mind can do with something more than this.

This also goes back to the priming topic I touched upon in the previous chapter: this is where our thinking is predisposed to flow due to recent exposure to a similar item, idea, view, etc. There was an almost infinite number of ways the crystal wand, coffee shop, locket, or sunglasses could be interpreted based on what we are primed/predisposed to believe. In the case of Sheldon and Amy, all the clues were seen through the prism of their recent marriage and new life together. This is what they chose to believe. And, herein lies the big lesson of this chapter - we very often chose to believe in something. Not because it is logical, not because we have evidence for it, but simply because we choose to believe it.

Now I do concede that this is a bold statement to make. Choosing one thing over another is suggestive of a willful and conscious decision. Very often, we do not believe something as a result of a conscious thought process. On the contrary, we are predisposed to do so based on a collection of pre-held believes, ideas, and experiences. Seen in this way, it is not surprising that we can all interpret a set of events in a completely different way.

Let's look at one of my favourite examples to illustrate the point, but I will modify it to make it a little more relevant in the wake of the COVID pandemic. COVID hits the world, and, sadly, a million people die. This can be seen in several different ways, depending on whom you ask. A devout religious believer might see this as a god's punishment of mankind for the many who live in sin because everything happens by God's will. A pragmatist could see this as something normal, just one of those things which happen from time to time. For a perennial conspiracy theorist, this would be a sinister plan for world domination, a method for mass control of the population, or a biological weapon test. A hedonist could interpret things as another reason to live life to the fullest because you might not be around tomorrow. YOLO! Similarly, a capitalist running a pharmaceutical company would be thrilled at the enormous opportunity to make billions out of the development and sale of vaccines. The list of possible interpretations is virtually endless.

There are a few logical conclusions I would like to draw at this point, before closing the chapter, and trust me, they are the real lessons learned:

1. Seek, and you shall find – if you look for meaning, you can always find one. My finance was recently telling me how she thought it was time for us to become parents

every time she saw a mother with a baby in the street. Is this a sign from the universe that perhaps it is time we had one of our own? I guess it is possible, but I am sure the universe has many more important things to do than sit there all day and contemplate what sign to send our way. At the end of the day, there are many thousands of babies in a city like London, so the likelihood of seeing one in the street is pretty high. See, if it is was a unicorn instead…

2. We interpret things differently – the exact same event could be perceived in very different ways by people based on our pre-held beliefs and experiences. Did you see the look on the face of that mother with her kid in the street? She looked desperate for a break. Maybe the universe is trying to tell us something completely different - we should stay away from kids because life is just too short to sacrifice while raising a child?

3. Don't judge people for believing one thing or another – we are all a by-product of our experiences and upbringing. If you were raised the same way as me and had somehow (make that miraculously) done and gone through everything the same way as me, in many cases, you would think like me too.

4. Sometimes, a glass of water is just that - a glass of water. Hard to believe, I know…

But who I am kidding? You will not remember any of this. I don't either. Lessons learned are incredibly over-rated and under-utilised. It is a mythical promise that we will be better and do things better next time, as if that next time is, at times, nothing more than an elusive goal. If only we were capable of learning…

13

Chapter 8 – Judging a Book by the Cover

"People don't really want to know anything about you. They just want you to fit into their little predetermined slots. They decide what you are in the first two seconds, and they only get nervous or upset if you don't live up to their snap judgments."
- Lilith Saintcrow

In the previous two chapters, we looked into our innate need to understand the world and why this is so important to us. In this chapter, we will cover the other big question – HOW do we do that. Which part of the brain is responsible for what decisions? Do we make snap decisions or carefully considered ones? Which is better? Altogether, this is a vast topic, and researchers have published countless papers on it.

My intention is not to delve into the merits of various experiments or even try to summarise everything that has been written on the topic for three reasons: 1) I am not a neuroscientist, 2) I will need a million years, and 3) this is completely irrelevant for the argument I intend to make in this chapter. For this book, my focus will be on one distinct part - snap judgements for one very simple reason – we hate it, we think we are better than this, and yet, and we do it all the time.

Snap judgements are decisions we make intuitively within a split second. It refers to the very first impression we get when we see someone or something, or as the British idiom puts it nicely – judge a book by the cover. Hopefully, reading the idiom has triggered a small negative reaction in your head. If it has, you're on the right track. It is exactly what I would expect, given that it is largely perceived with a negative connotation as something shallow, undesirable, and morally untenable. But is that even surprising? I have never heard anyone saying, "Judge this person or that action by the cover." It is always "don't judge", said with more than a tinge of animosity and spite in the voice, as if you are a vile creature that needs to be despised. Paradoxically, people would judge you for judging. Or perhaps, it is fine if they judge your judgement, something like killing a bad person. I shot him, but it is fine because he was a wrong person. So, in reality, I did a good thing.

There is a vast body of research into snap judgement, and scientists still cannot agree whether snap judgement is more often correct or reliable when compared with a slower, well-calibrated analysis. Research on this topic is predictably inconclusive as you have one scientist saying snap decisions are more accurate than the slower ones, whereas someone else will advocate the opposite. But the fact of life is that we use snap judgement, and I do mean all the time.

Snap judgement is critical for our survival and well-being. It allows us to make instantaneous decisions about people, objects, threats, etc. Research shows that it only takes us 0.05 seconds to make a decision[21]. This is pretty efficient, isn't it? Every time we encounter a new situation, person, or event, the process is triggered, which needs to be assessed immediately. Envision this situation – you start crossing a road while thinking about your shopping list and do not pay too much attention. In the very next moment, you hear a car honk and instinctively jump back on the pavement. It was your legs, which immediately spurred to action, but legs do not move alone. The command came from your brain, which processed the information and issued an order. It all happened within a split second. In this situation, you do not have much time to assess the threat and make a more informed decision. Imagine standing in the middle of the road, while the brain is trying to calculate the vehicle's speed coming towards you against the distance to impact, and decipher what the driver will do. Will he jump on the breaks immediately or just signal and carry on? If the former, will the stopping distance be short enough to avoid the impact, etc. By the time you work this out, you are possibly gone.

As we have seen with many other cognitive processes so far, snap judgements also go back to pre-historical times and have played a major role in preserving mankind. It is, after all, a survival mechanism. If our caveman Ken met a tiger, which was charging towards him, he wouldn't be standing there, trying to work out if the tiger liked him and just wanted to play, or if his stone tip spear could pierce the animal's skin in case the tiger fancied him more as a meal rather than a game buddy. Remember the simple rule – you see a tiger charging towards you, run with all you got, and hope it still carries some extra weight since last Christmas. Just for reference, in case you decide to fight it, a male tiger weighs around 300kg, and its paw is strong enough to crash a bull's skull with a single swing. In case you still fancy your chances, I read that tigers were less likely to kill you if you stared them in the eyes. Good luck, and may your soul rest in peace!

But, this is not a chapter about tigers or what to do if one attacks you; it is about making snap decisions. One could think that while snap decisions might be required in certain cases, how often do we find ourselves in a life-or-death situation when such instantaneous judgement is exactly what you need? Not that often, and thank God for that. However, my larger point is that these rather extreme examples are being made to illustrate the fact that we invoke our "snap brains" in a lot more mundane situations daily – every time we meet someone personally or even see them in the street, notice a dog running in the park, register a car driving towards us even if in the distance, or walk around a building site. In each of these and many other cases, we visually perceive the new element and make an instantaneous decision if it constitutes a threat. This is not a part of deliberate thinking; it usually happens subconsciously.

So far, so good. But one pertinent question remains – how do we know whether or not a perceived threat awaits us? As fascinating as our brains are, they are no prophets. There is no way of knowing for sure whether the gentle-looking man walking towards us won't pull a gun out and start shooting at random, or whether the blue car will not hit us after suddenly steering onto the pavement. However, our brains can certainly look for clues, potentially suggesting if something could be off – trajectory, posture, speed, nervousness, sudden movements, outfit, facial expressions, etc. In the previous chapters, we have already seen how we can draw conclusions based on partial information. This is a prime example of snap judgement. We use whatever information available, however incomplete, to form a quick judgement.

Like I mentioned at the beginning of this chapter, there is a fair amount of disagreement on this topic, but let's be realistic here, we cannot expect this cognitive process to be flawless. There just isn't enough information we can derive within a split second to consistently draw the correct conclusion. Imagine standing at the centre of a busy shopping mall, with hundreds of people walking around, escalators constantly moving up and down, boisterous kids running, and loud music playing from the speakers. At the same time, you hear fragments of various indistinct conversations, promotional banners, and signs flashing everywhere... if this is not sensory overload, I don't know what is. If you had to stand there and carefully assess everything to increase the snap judgement's reliability, you would go insane before you're able to process all this information. In this context, judgement is nothing more than a mental shortcut our brains employ to assess the environment to ensure our wellbeing and convenience, even at the expense of some reliability.

With this in mind, it is not surprising that we judge by the cover all the time; we are simply wired this way. When we meet someone for the first time, whether in a social environment or at work, we immediately form an opinion about them, based on how they are dressed, their posture, their facial features, voice, etc. This transmits plenty of credible information – are they likely to be trustworthy or not, are they likely to be good at their job or not, are they posing some sort of threat to us or not. We look at their shoes, watch, phone, or car to assess their social status – are they poor or well off. We conclude various characteristics – affluence, reliability, character, knowledge, professionalism, and a lot more. Depending on the setting wherein we meet someone, we might be looking for different clues. If you are going on a first date with someone, you will likely notice their appearance first. Do they look healthy; how tall are they (women generally prefer men who are taller than them); do they look confident or are they sweating and shaking already (confidence is a big bonus for many people); how are they dressed; is the hair nice and tidy or is it dishevelled (a tidy hair could suggest more effort was put in or that the person is organised, while a messy hair on the side could imply otherwise or maybe have some unique style). If you meet someone for a business meeting, you will probably look for very different characteristics. How are they dressed? A suit and a tie for a man or an elegant dress, or a suit for a woman always make a good first impression. Are they on time or late; how young or old is the person; and so on. Rightly or wrongly, this is linked to how informed or knowledgeable they are perceived to be. You will probably prefer doing business or are more likely to take advice from a seasoned expert with seemingly 20-30 years of experience than a young guy, who looks like he has come straight out of uni. Yes, the cues could vary from one person to another, but they are always there. We all know someone who first looks at either the shoes, the watch, or the handbag when meeting a new person.

All of this happens quickly and automatically, leveraging some pre-conceptions we cultivate in our heads about a particular characteristic being more desirable than another. We have built a little mental cheat sheet throughout our lives, which propels snap judgements. Again, it could differ from one person to another, but it could be something like:

Undesirable characteristics:

Short, unattractive, jeans and t-shirt (in a business environment), random university degree, common accent, etc.

Desirable characteristics:

Tall, attractive, expensive watch, suit shirt and tie (in a business environment), Oxbridge degree, posh accent, etc.

This is just an example, but we all have our preferences or preconceptions regarding the desirability of certain characteristics, be it from our taste or societal and cultural preferences. Upon encountering these characteristics, they immediately signal to our brains. As I mentioned before, this is not necessarily a fully reliable cognitive system, and first impressions can often be misleading. But, once again, the point here is not whether it is reliable or not. We have evolved to give preference to speed and ease of processing information over reliability. It makes for an efficient but not necessarily a perfect cognitive model. That doesn't matter. All that matters is understanding our proclivity to form judgements based on first impressions and, where possible, question it. It is not something we can change but armed with this understanding. We can indeed take steps to refine this process and build a more realistic and truthful picture of the world.

14

Chapter 9 - Snap Decisions and Prejudice

"If we were to wake up some morning and find that everyone was the same race, creed, and color, we would find some other causes for prejudice by noon."
- George Aiken

WARNING – skip this chapter if you happen to be overly sentimental or find it hard to swallow a bitter pill called truth. You are likely to encounter the latter and experience the former. Okay, so now that we've gotten our customary disclaimer out of the way, let's dive straight in!

This chapter will look at some of the underlying beliefs and prejudices that underpin snap decisions. I will touch on a few undeniably sensitive areas (an understatement), which means it is more than likely to ruffle some feathers. So, proceed with care.

In the previous chapter, we looked at some simple examples of judging a book by the cover – whether or not someone is attractively looking, how they are dressed, how expensive or cheap their belongings are, and so on. These proclivities barely scratch the surface of decision-making or even snap judgements, but at the end of the day, this is EXACTLY where snap judgements thrive – on the surface.

But, how do we know if something or someone is good or bad? Let's say we come across a guy wearing a hoodie fighting in the street; would we construe him as a good person or an evil fellow? We see a father in the street with this lightly dressed young son; will he be seen as a bad father for not being too cold and indifferent to put an extra layer on his son in this cold weather? We see a scruffy-looking man rushing to the tube station with messy hair, dirty shoes, and an untucked shirt; what would we make of him? A mother is queuing up at the counter in a large grocery store just in front of us, and her shopping cart is loaded with chips, pizza, pre-cooked meals, and all kinds of frozen foods. Does she even care about the health of her children?

Let's try and get to the bottom of things. In each of these cases, our penchant for pre-conceived notions or pre-held beliefs is brought to the fore. We have been cultivating these all our lives without even knowing about them. We associate guys wearing hoodies with thugs, and the guy fighting only reinforces the presumption that he could be a bad person or even a criminal. We associate cold weather with warm clothes, so a father who has not dressed his son appropriately for this weather cannot be a particularly good father. Scruffy, dirty, messy all carry negative connotations, so seeing someone matching this description immediately influences our attitude towards this person. Junk food is generally accepted as unhealthy and linked to various health-related issues, which is why we assume that a mother feeding her children with such food is bound to be ignominiously ignorant and careless.

And this is the key thing here – we hold beliefs, feelings, and preconceptions towards everything we know. We are born (almost) a blank sheet of paper, which we fill in throughout our lives with knowledge and experiences. Some of these will be subjective and sometimes wrong, but we have already discussed the efficacy of instilling mental shortcuts, establishing patterns, generalisation, etc. They are a necessary evil for us to function properly as humans. Some of these attitudes are quite obvious, and we are painstakingly aware of them, whereas others are a lot more subtle, implicit, and even subconscious.

If you had to categorise the following words into two broad categories, "good" or "bad", where would you place them?

GOOD	BAD
Tall	
Short	
Pretty	
Ugly	

Now think about these two hypothetical questions:

1. Is a tall person more or less likely to be better at their job than a short person?
2. Should a more attractive criminal receive a more favourable sentence than a less attractive one, who has committed a similar crime?

At a surficial level, the answer to both questions should be, "it should not matter; height and physical appearance are completely irrelevant in both cases." You are right, but you are also wrong! It should not matter, but it does.

A vast body of research shows that taller people are more likely to be promoted or generally be successful in their careers. Height is a cue for socioeconomic status and better education. One research on over 120 000 people in the UK suggested that tall men earn on average £2940 more annually compared to similarly qualified shorter colleagues[22]. Similarly, a poll conducted by Malcolm Gladwell, the author of the New York Times best-seller *Blink: The power of thinking without thinking,* shows that tall people are more likely to get to a CEO position of a Fortune 500 company. According to his findings, while a mere 14.5% of the US population is above 6 feet tall, this percentage jumps to 58% among CEOs of Fortune 500 companies[23]. So, if you are a tall person, congratulations, you are more likely to succeed in the workplace (apparently, the height prejudice is more pronounced for men than women). I have known of this prejudice towards tall men for a long time and have made a conscious effort to look at Managing Directors in my company. Indeed, the majority of MDs I know are quite tall, and many of them are taller than me (and I am of average height). Now it does not hold true for every company, but it is a curious observation nonetheless.

Similarly, there are multiple pieces of research looking into the objectiveness of judges and, more specifically, the impact of the criminals' physical attractiveness on the severity of their sentence. It blows my mind when I see that more attractive criminals tend to get away with a lot less punitive sentences. Attractive people, you see, are generally perceived as more intelligent, moral, and altruistic with more appealing personalities[24]. All this goes to say is that, while more skilled at judging character, judges are susceptible to biases and impressions like every other person. Highly trained and knowledgeable they might be, they are also humans.

At this stage, it is probably evident that no person can reasonably justify better performance at work with height (unless in certain professions like boxing, for example, where height can give one an important edge), and no judge will admit that they passed a more favourable verdict because they liked the defendant's sparkling blue eyes. These influences are subtle and deeply unconscious.

So far, this chapter has not been too bad... but things are about to get uglier—last warning.

If we hold certain beliefs about height, weight, dress code, and appearance, which influence our attitudes and perceptions of people, what else could be out there? I am afraid I am going to have to spell it out– so do race, gender, religion, sexual orientation, etc. All of these are extremely sensitive topics, to say the least.

I wanted to cover these here because discriminating on these grounds is unethical, widely stigmatised, and condemned in modern societies. While this is rightfully the case, it often gets to a point where the mere use of the word "black" or even making a factual comparison like "men are genetically taller than women" is enough to offend or infuriate someone. We have all gone too sensitive as a society, way beyond what is normal or healthy. Is it just me thinking that? Before I say anything, I have to think five times to avoid inadvertently offending someone... not that it helps me much... If that wasn't bad enough, we live in a deeply hypocritical society that would openly and publicly condemn one's slightest reference to race, gender, or sexual orientation, anyone's ability to do anything, etc., intentional, or not, while covertly harbouring similar beliefs.

There is no denying that racism and bigotry are still an integral part of society and must be obliterated. What most people do not realise, however, is that we all are part of the problem. Remember the example with the out-of-stock toilet paper at the beginning of COVID, where we would condemn those people who decided to stockpile it while aggravating the problem ourselves by overstocking due to misplaced hysteria and paranoia? The problem here is similar – we are part of the same society that would openly stigmatise racism, only to snub the next black person who we have to interview for a job, tutor at school, or examine medically. I understand that these are all very grave accusations, but first, I am also part of this same society, and second, like it or not, I am merely stating what plenty of research proves. Many people would disagree with some of the statements I am making in this chapter. This is as expected for two key reasons: one – it hurts us to think we could hold prejudices against certain groups because we realise it is immoral; two – very often, we do not even realise it that we do, it is subconscious.

It is important to distinguish between explicit and implicit beliefs. Explicit beliefs are those we choose to hold and express openly. A simple example would be – "I do believe that all people, regardless of skin colour, sex, political and religious beliefs, height, weight, social class, profession, etc., are equal and deserve equal treatment." There are, however, implicit beliefs, those who lurk underneath the surface, those we have adopted as we go along and might uphold without even realising it. I would argue these are a lot more truthful, as they are not self-proclaimed but can be observed scientifically.

In 1995, two social psychology researchers, Anthony Greenwald and Mahzarin Banaji, introduced a test called Implicit Association Test (IAT) to explore the strength of commonly-held subconscious associations[25]. This test has since been widely used to assess the strength of various implicit stereotypes around race, gender, age, sexual orientation, etc. The tests are straightforward– you are given pictures and/or words, which you are asked to categorise while recording and calculating the speed of response. The key principle behind the test is that we are faster at categorising words or images, which align with our pre-existing beliefs and associations. Here is an example.

In a race test, you are given a series of words, split into "good" and "bad" e.g.:

Good: cheerful, triumph, joyful, magnificent, cheer, pleasing, fantastic, excellent

Bad: annoy, rotten, pain, disgust, yucky, sadness, dirty, humiliate

Then you are asked to assign them to one of two categories, as shown below.

Scenario 1:

Press "E" for
Bad
or
African Americans

Press "I" for
Good
or
European Americans

Pain

Scenario 2:

Press "E" for
Bad
or
White people

Press "I" for
Good
or
Black people

Abuse

Note that the difference between the two scenarios is the grouping. In scenario 1, white people are grouped with good and black people with bad. Meanwhile, in scenario 2, white people are grouped with bad, black people with good.

For people, who hold pro-white people prejudice, the response time in scenario 1 would be shorter than in scenario 2. This is because they would subconsciously be associating white people with good, so they would not need to think as long about it.

This and many other tests are available to do for free on the following website: https://implicit.harvard.edu/implicit/education.html, but beware, results can be quite upsetting.

The overwhelming evidence from this test is that most of us have implicit prejudice against discriminated groups. We have all heard of deplorable instances or statistics about people being discriminated against in one way or another. The examples are countless, but I will share just a few here.

1. One study discovered that when applying for a job, black applicants were half as likely to be called in for an interview compared to white applicants with similar qualifications. This is the result of both explicit and implicit bias[26].
2. Another research has found a huge racial disparity in how black defendants are treated in criminal sentencing, impacting everything from initial police contact all the way through to passing a sentence[27].
3. In the US, the labour force participation of people with disabilities was mere 20.9% in 2018, compared to 68.3% for people without disabilities[28].
4. In light of the COVID outbreak, prejudice has also appeared against Asians. In the pre-COVID months, 77% of Asian men with a high school degree in the US were reportedly working. This was 6% higher than similarly educated white men (71%). In the second quarter of 2020, however, the employment rate among these Asians fell by 31%, compared to 9% for whites[29]. The

adoption of anti-Asian sentiments can only explain such disparity following the COVID spread. I guess President Trump calling it the "China virus" did not help, either.
5. In 2017 one in five LGBT people experienced a hate crime in the UK due to their sexual orientation. What is alarming is that every four in five cases are not even reported out of fear they would not be taken seriously[30].

The fact is that while prejudice and discrimination continue to be a massive challenge for various groups and classes, this only explains *part* of the unemployment rates for disabled people, part of the discrepancy in the level of care towards white and black kids in schools, *part* of the disparities in the level of attention by doctors towards white and minority patients, *part* of the extra severe verdicts and sentences some minorities receive, *part* of the male-dominated corporate boards, etc.

I am trying to clarify how many of us hold implicit prejudice towards various groups, which contributes to the wider issues in our societies. Inadvertently, many of us would be responsible for those same problems we publicly condemn. There are various reasons for this. I will list a few of the more common ones that affect us all.

I have already mentioned that we are born a blank sheet of paper. No baby is born with genetic or innate mistrust or prejudices toward the opposite sex, other races, religions, or whatever societal groups you can think of. We pick these up as we go along. Our upbringing and the society in which we are raised through the formative years of our lives dramatically impact the beliefs we acquire. And we are all raised slightly differently. What our parents believe, what our teachers believe and pass onto us, the area or country we have grown up into, the school we attended, the people we have met in our lives, the kind of TV programmes we watch, all of these influences collectively determine the person we will become. If we have grown up in a neighbourhood that is generally diverse and inclusive of all races, genders, and sexual orientations, we would inexorably be comfortable around these people and perceive them as equals from the start. This is one of the benefits of living in a large and diverse city like London. You can meet all kinds of people, which generally tends to promote equality. On the other hand, if you have grown up in a country where gay marriages are unlawful or society ostracizes people in same-sex relationships, you are more likely to adopt homophobic beliefs.

Historical roots play an equally important role in all of this. It is curious that US states, which historically had higher slavery rates, today have higher prejudice levels towards the black population than those where slavery was not as widespread or accepted[31]. History often leaves an indelible impression on people's cultural attitudes and beliefs. I am not particularly proud to say that my native country Bulgaria is consistently ranked among the worst countries in corruption. It is widespread, and the reasons are multifarious, but one of the key factors is its communist past. Up until 1989, like many other Eastern European countries, Bulgaria was a communist state, which structurally and culturally favours corruptive practices. This was over 30 years ago now, but people who have been running the country since then are a product of the communist ethos, which has left a mark on their beliefs and behaviour.

This is a nice segue into my next and the last point – changing the mindset of a society is a long and painful process. Rome wasn't built in a day. A meaningful sociocultural transformation cannot take place overnight. The world is transitioning towards a lot more liberal and equal state, and it has been for a long time. The various movements for equality have started an irreversible trend to a world without racism, homophobia, or bigotry, with battles won every day, but it will take many more years until we get there. The people who rule the world now are the same people who were raised in a different time themselves, when the internet was not that ubiquitous and even non-existent in some places, a time when society was a lot more narrow-minded. A real change can only gain a foothold for good owing to the resilience and perseverance of equality movements. The onus is on us to uphold the principles we currently espouse to promise a better tomorrow.

15

Chapter 10 – We Only See Black and White

"We're so quick to go to make things black and white, and to put things in their box. But everything is this mixture, and that's what this world is, is this blend of different things."
- Matthew Miller (Matisyahu)

One thing you might have noticed in the last two chapters is the binary nature of the groupings and categorisations that were used in many of the examples: good vs. bad, tall vs. short, desirable vs. undesirable, attractive vs. unattractive, etc. This is a nice prelude to the topic I would cover in this chapter – the binary fashion in which we perceive and categorise things. We tend to view things as black and white (and no, I am not referring to race or skin colour), and rarely grey. This propensity is just another heuristic our minds have learned to regularly employ. It really is fascinating how many different techniques our minds use in the background to let us get on with our lives without being paralysed with choices, options, and decisions.

Think about the following question – "Am I a good person?" Sounds simple enough, doesn't it? The likelihood is, you, like me, would answer with a definitive "yes". We already spoke about our blind spots when it comes to our own faults and shortcomings, which would obviously tip the scale in favour of "yes" for most people, but the answer here is not even important. What is important for this chapter are the following two things:

1. This is such a nebulous question that we could define the criteria as we see fit to help our case. A hundred people could come up with a hundred different criteria, which define a good person: upholding the values of our religion, being a law-abiding citizen, being benevolent towards our family or friends, not drinking excessively or taking drugs, not cheating on our partner, offering a seat to an elderly person or a pregnant woman on the bus, donating to charity, being respectful to everyone around us…the list is virtually endless.
2. Regardless of how we define being a good or a bad person, the likelihood is we will not tick every single box. i.e., always doing the honourable and righteous thing and never anything bad or ill-intentioned. Most of us

could find some examples to add to the "bad boy/girl" category. When I say "some", I am really thinking "all", but will give people the benefit of the doubt. The bottom line is, we are a mixture of good and bad i.e., we are a shade of grey. How dark or light this shade is, though, is very individual.

These two observations are important because they show the real nature of the world we live in – it is vague and complex, never just black or white. We can observe this in many cases and examples around us – should I get married or not? Should I invest money, time, and effort in writing a book, which might not sell? Should I keep my current job or look for another one? Should I pick up hiking? There will always be arguments for and against. So, what should we decide? The standard approach to this would be to weigh the pros and cons of each option and pick the best one. You do not need an Excel spreadsheet for this, in most cases it is just a mental list. Whichever option you then pick, however, encapsulates all the good and the bad of this decision.

In the previous chapters, we mentioned our innate need to draw conclusions explaining the world around us. We also covered the mental shortcuts allowing us to draw these conclusions and more importantly doing it quickly and efficiently (not necessarily always correctly). We might have supercomputers in our heads, but these are by no means omnipotent or flawless. When we give this computer vast amounts of data to process (often conflicting data) and want the result now, it is bound to employ some shortcuts, which would inevitably lead to lower quality of the output. In this respect, our brains are not much different from humans when our boss comes over and wants us to do A, B, C D, E, F, and G... TODAY! Welcome to cutting corners.

Our brains do not like complexity or working very hard, for that matter. Extraordinary as they are, there are certain limitations, so dealing with vague, uncertain, or complex scenarios, would require two things: structure and simplification (that is, the cutting corners part). The two things are intrinsically related, as the structure would instil clarity and simplicity. This is not surprising because it comes naturally to us. I have often heard people saying, "you cannot generalise", with a note of judgement in the voice. This is one of the things I hate hearing the most, simply because it is utter nonsense. Groupings, simplifications, and generalisations are all constructs that allow us to cut through the chaos and formulate a simpler, more comprehensive conclusion. They are nothing more than mental shortcuts, and we all use them. Yes, not everything and everyone fit into the same box, yes, there are always exceptions, but when we talk about patterns or categories, we care about the majority of subjects falling into this category, not the minority or exceptions. Think about those simple statements.

- **I like chocolate**. This, of course, is a generalisation. I like most types of chocolate, but not dark chocolate with mint flavour. Yuck! But when I am asked if I like choco-

late, I wouldn't start listing every single type I like or dislike, and nor would you.
- **Why are you always late?** The likelihood is imaginary person X is not late every single time, but the statement generalises a pattern or a frequent occurrence.
- **Teenagers these days are addicted to their phones.** Maybe your niece Maria is an exception to this rule, and she prefers reading books instead, but generally, most teenagers nowadays would fall into this category.

All of this is important to express a view simply and comprehensively. Imagine you are a sales analyst in a big consumer goods company. The sales director has organised a meeting with the various divisions to go through the sales for the last quarter, and you need to present the performance of your division. Behind your analysis, there are thousands of rows of data coming from various disparate systems. Product A sold this many items via this channel; product B's sales were up by 330 items compared to the previous quarter; product C's sales plummeted due to a marginal price increase; and the prices of products D, E, and F were cut down, etc. You have all these data at your fingertips, but the manager wouldn't care about all the details. They want to know the story, the highlights, and the big picture. Our brains are structured similarly - to separate the wheat from the chaff and focus on what matters – a simple narrative: are the sales good or are they not.

To add another aspect, most qualitative and quantitative criteria in this world can be seen as a continuum. Let's consider a simple example of human height. We would normally think of people as tall or short because it is simpler. In reality, however, height is a continuum. The world's tallest person as of Jan 2021, is a Turkish man called Sultan Kösen, holding a Guinness World Record with his impressive 251 cm (or 8 ft 2 in). In comparison, the shortest person in the world is an Indian lady called Jyoti Amge, who is barely 62.8 cm tall (2f 0.6 in) and four times shorter than Mr. Kösen. The rest of the human population would fall somewhere in between. However, there are just too many variations between the two extremes for us to realistically register or be even practical to use, so we would usually use a heuristic to split people into two categories: tall or short. Or maybe tall, short, and average height. These categories are relative and could be valued differently by different people i.e., person A might consider above 180 cm as tall, person B – above 190 cm, person C – above 200, and so on.

Take another example – bananas. Are they healthy or not? Well, you cannot argue with the fact that they're a source of fibre, vitamins, and potassium, an electrolyte helping to regulate the heart rate and blood pressure. So, I would say they are. However, if you eat a truckload of bananas, you could overdose on potassium and make your heart stop. It is an extreme example, as realistically speaking, no one can eat this many bananas, but it is an interesting theoretical question nonetheless – at which point do bananas stop being healthy and become unhealthy?

One last example – imagine you are reading a newspaper and you see the following headline – "A woman sentenced for shoplifting milk and eggs from her local store". You are yet to read the article, but what do you think the moment you read this headline? Here are a few possibilities:

1. God, what is wrong with people?
2. Really? Milk and eggs? If you would be stealing, at least make it count.
3. What a low life!
4. Oh no, that's horrible.

There's an implicit judgement in each of these thoughts. It isn't hard to see why one would think that. Shoplifting is, of course, unethical and unlawful, so you would be quick to condemn the act. Then you also add the petty factor there – it was milk and eggs. Who would be so petty to shoplift something so generic and cheap? You know nothing about the woman and are already thinking the worst of her – petty shoplifter, that's all she is! But then you start reading the article itself, and a few important facts surface. Let's just call the woman – Emily for ease. So, Emily is a single mother, raising her two young kids by herself. She has been trying really hard, but the hair-dresser salon where she works hasn't been doing too well lately. To save costs, the owner decided to reduce the work hours of existing staff, hence cutting Emily's total pay. She has more time for her children but less money. Between rent, bills, and regular expenditures for food, she has been struggling to make both ends meet lately. Her credit card is maxed out, she also owes friends money, so there's no way she will borrow more from them. She gave whatever money that was left with her to pay rent to keep the roof above her family's heads. What do you do when your kids - the most important thing for a mother-are hungry again and you have run out of options? What would you do in this case?

It is a very bleak scenario, but unfortunately, a frequent reality for some people. Life is not a bed of roses for most people. The problem is, unless it is us in those shoes, from a third-party perspective, we see too little to appreciate all of this complexity and what drives people to do what they do. As I illustrated in a previous chapter, this hardly ever stops us from drawing a conclusion. We work with what we have at hand, sufficient or not. This is supported by our need for a simple and consistent explanation. This is perfectly normal for us and our brains. Indubitably, it isn't a particularly flattering feature of how we are structured. It opens us to drawing incorrect conclusions or often failing to consider all nuances or factors at play. We do no do this particularly well, but this is the price we have to pay when living in a complex world.

Have you ever listened to a market analyst, an economist or an "expert" in any area talking about the latest market crash, or the outcome of a political or economic decision? They always seem to have all the answers, don't they? This political decision led to that happening. The share price of company X went up or down by 20% because... The latest measures concerning combating the COVID pandemic proved unsuccessful because... The government's decision to deploy troops in this region, did not have the intended benefits, while it cost the taxpayers X amount of money, which was obvious from the beginning... There is one common denominator here – all of this analysis comes after the effect. This often shows that we are not particularly good at predicting the future, but we are particularly good at explaining the past. This goes back to complexity. At the point of making a decision, there are always arguments for and against, like I mentioned at the beginning of this chapter. It is very often hard...or even impossible to predict what will happen in the future and the exact outcome of a decision. This is one of the properties of complexity. Instead, it is much easier to justify an outcome by cherry picking all those arguments in support of it, as if it was obvious all along...and look smart in the process. All we can do is give our best estimate and hope we will turn out right.

This chapter is trying to demonstrate that we are not particularly good at appreciating or factoring in complexity in everyday situations. This is one of the shortcomings of our fast brains. Evolution has favoured efficiency over completeness. As I will explore further in the following chapters, our brains are exceptionally energy-intensive organs, and if they are to function properly in an age of information overload, they need to streamline their functioning, even if at the expense of some reliability. It would have been amazing if they could be perfect – always rational, always sensible, having perfect information, and being able to untangle complexity within a split second, but again, it just isn't that simple. So, making simplifying assumptions, categorising and generalising, which inevitably lead to a loss of some of the information, are just some of the techniques we need to leverage to continue functioning as normal humans.

16

Section 3 – It Is All Coming Together

The first two sections of this book focused on ego and heuristics. They are two very different concepts as the former has a lot to do with how we feel about certain things, while the latter has more to do with our thought. Yet, they are both very important as often complementary, but also, together, they lay the foundations for many of our attitudes and behaviours towards everything around us. We will see them coming back as highlights throughout the rest of the book, as we are adding more nuances to the complex puzzle that the human psyche is.

17

Chapter 11 – Perceiving the World Differently

"What is behind your eyes holds more power than what is in front of them."
- Gary Zukav

This chapter will look into perceptions, how we perceive the world, how perceptions differ among people, and how they drive our behaviour. This is an important topic because perceptions are very subjective and have a huge impact on our thoughts and actions. So, what we do, what we think or say is strongly determined by whom we are, leading to a virtually unlimited combination of actions. Yet, we expect people to behave in a particular way, in congruence with what is deemed socially acceptable i.e., we create expectations and very often end up ignoring the personal and subjective side of things.

If I asked you– "Are people all the same or each one of us is unique in our own way?", what would you say? Generally, most people would strongly agree and say yes. We are all unique, and no two people are completely alike. We can expand that, which means we all think, feel, and behave differently, and that everyone is free to be themselves. This is the richness and beauty of our species; we are, after all, almost eight billion unique individuals. Despite this conscious agreement, we often expect people to fit a particular stereotype of behaviour. I can only describe that as bounded uniqueness i.e., we can be unique within certain boundaries, and very often, these boundaries are quite narrow. This reminds me of the famous Henry Ford saying about its famous Model T, "Any customer can have a car painted any colour that he wants, so long as it is black."[32]

In reality, we do not like attitudes or behaviours (and, by extension, perceptions), which are too dissimilar to ours. Think about your group of friends. Do you share similar perceptions and beliefs or are you all different? In you and your friends are like most of us, you are quite likely the former type. I would like to take this a step further and make a bold statement – this holds true for companies too. Companies these days love talking about diversity and how many nationalities they represent. They love saying how their diverse workforce is a source of competitive advantage and one of the driving forces behind their success. While this is certainly the case and, diversity is important from an organisational perspective, I dare say that many companies could not care less about diversity. It is all a cheap PR trick, which bodes well with media and shareholders or has been reduced to a tick-box exercise. Diversity is important so long as it fits a model and a popular opinion or as Ford would put it, "so long as it is black." Once your opinion is no longer compatible with the agreed model, your cultural advantage turns you into being seen as "difficult", "unsupportive of the ideas of the company", and "uncollaborative". This is the unfortunate, even if cynical, truth for too many companies today, but let's pull back to the main topic before I do on to hurt too many feelings.

As a foreigner living in the UK, the difference in perceptions is particularly close to my heart. I am sure many fellow foreigners around the world could probably relate to this too, as cultural differences form a large part of the way we perceive information and our unique identities. As an Eastern European living in Western Europe, I have witnessed or have been involved in countless such situations. In Eastern Europe, people are more direct, honest, and open about their thoughts and feelings than in many Western societies. Inevitably, this often makes us be perceived as insensitive or outright rude. Twelve years in the UK have certainly softened my expressions a lot, but I still sometimes find myself in situations when after a comment of mine, people awkwardly look at each other thinking, "How could he say that?" Lashing out against pseudo corporate diversity is a great example of that. Ooops, I did it again! More on that later in the chapter.

Perceptions are an interesting thing. We can all see, hear, or smell the same thing but perceive it very differently. However, we hardly ever think about that because we simply expect everyone to perceive information in the same way we do. If we see a red rose in the garden, it is just a red rose in the garden. I see it, and everyone else who looks at it would see the same thing. We are not designed to question what we see or perceive, and by extension, do not usually question if anyone else perceives the same thing as us. The thing is, seeing and perceiving are not the same thing. In the above example, we can all see a flower, but how we think of it could be very different. Person A could look at it and see just that – a rose, barely registering it and moving on. Person B could look at the same thing but perceive the flower as a beautiful little piece of nature in the big concrete jungle that we allude to as a city. It might even cause him to feel incensed at all the mindless urbanisation and its impact on nature. Person C could suddenly start feeling emotional due to this being the favourite flower of their now-deceased dear relative, standing there for a few seconds while overwhelmed with treasured memories, and so on. This is perfectly captured by the Gary Zukav quote I have included at the beginning of this chapter that what's behind our eyes holds more power than what is in front of them.

But why do we perceive things differently?

Our brains are incessantly, almost mercilessly inundated with information overload. They cannot cope and process it all, so a lot of this incoming information is filtered out while the rest is retained and registered. This is a perfectly natural process, but here is where things get interesting. How does the brain decide what information to retain and what to discard? Science tells us that it does that based on what it considers important or relevant based on our personality, attitudes, and former experiences. Because they are all unique, the retained information also tends to be unique. But hang on, there's more that you need to know. Once the relevant bit of information is selected, it needs to be processed to a meaningful conclusion. Once again, things are not just black and white. While this is a mechanical and subconscious process for us, the information is analysed and understood against our cultural and behavioural characteristics and experiences. If I can express this process visually, it would be something like that.

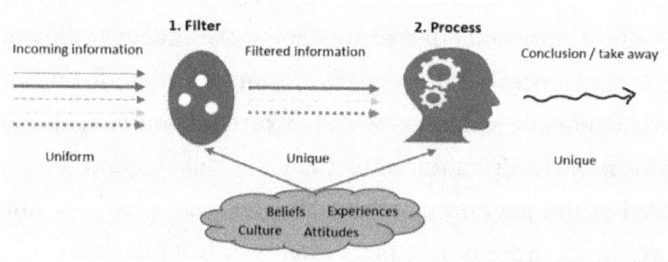

It is pivotal to understand that perception is a two-way road. It is as much external information coming in as a reflection of what's inside us, but we're often unmindful of this. We tend to focus more on the incoming information and its source than the return link and those factors, specific to us, which impact how this information is processed and understood. It is a situation I have observed frequently when a break in communication results in a good old-fashioned misunderstanding between individuals. This is not entirely surprising as it is always easier to blame others than question our own actions or beliefs (we will talk more about this specifically later in the book). It's time for some more examples!

So, we have a few friends – Persons A, B, C and D. Person A goes, "Jack and I went out a couple of times last week. We went for a meal at this Italian restaurant on Tuesday evening and once again for a few drinks on Friday with some of his work colleagues. It felt quite nice to have a meal and some drinks out, for a change. It has been a long and boring lockdown after all." Quite a harmless and mundane conversation between friends, isn't it? However, the message it conveys can be decoded very differently by Persons B, C and D. Person B, who has been having some financial difficulties lately, cannot help but think, "Can't she stop bragging about going out? Not everyone has the means to go out even once, let alone twice a week. How can she be so insensitive?" Next, Person B complains to her other friends about how vain and inconsiderate Person A was. Now, Person A might not have had any ulterior motives other than sharing her happiness with her friend.

On the surface, there is nothing wrong or offensive with her comment either. The problem comes from the way Person B decoded this message, because she understood it in light of her situation and experience, more specifically seen through the prism of her beleaguered financial situation, which has been on her mind recently. In contrast, Person C, who had suffered severely from COVID a few months back, is infuriated by the lack of mindfulness displayed by Person A. "It is this kind of people who made this COVID pandemic so much worse. How could she not have any regard for other people's health? Just stay at home, for God's sake", they might think. And then, we have Person D, who is a good friend of Person A and does not read much into this. She is just glad her friend had a good time. It is the same message but spurring such a stark contrast of responses...

Factors influencing our perceptions

Several factors influence the way we perceive information, both verbally and visually. Let's briefly review some of the common ones.

1. Culture – culture has many different manifestations – the way we talk, how much we drink, what we eat, how close we stand to each other, etc. For example, people in some countries are a lot more open and candid about their feelings/opinions. From my experience, Eastern Europeans and Filipinos are a lot more likely to tell you what they think about you than the British, for ex-

ample. The former would see this as honesty, which is generally a desirable personality trait, even though it might offend someone. Yet, this can be seen as insensitive in other cultures. British, on the other side, who are known for their politeness, would tiptoe around the truth and smile politely even though they often feel differently. This is seen as polite, sensitive, or politically correct.

2. Past experiences – we all have some baggage we carry from earlier experiences. We may have been abused or bullied at school, our parents may have divorced, or we may have bad memories (or lack of) from vodka on a Saturday night 15 years ago, we had our home broken into or always used to go for a walk in the park with our grandparents, some experiences leave a mark. They would later reflect on how we think of certain events or ideas.

3. Psychological state – we can perceive things very differently based on what time of day it is or what mood we are in. We are more likely to appreciate the funny side of things if we are in a relaxing atmosphere, feel well, or have other people around us than if the opposite was true. I have noticed my sense of humour is a lot more prominent earlier in the day and on weekends when I am well rested than after a long day at work, after which I just want to sit in front of the TV and open a beer.

4. Environment – our environment is often more important than anything else. People are generally more likely

to laugh out loud during a comedy movie when watching with friends and family than alone. Men work harder in the gym when a pretty woman is around (and that's a fact!). We go to a comedy show where someone stands in front of us and has the temerity to mock us on cultural, religious, sexual, and any other grounds imaginable, while we laugh as if we're having the time of our life. Those same 'jokes' surely won't be as funny in the office or at a Christmas dinner with the in-laws.

The key points I am trying to make are as follows: 1) who we are, has a lot more to do with the way we understand the world than we appreciate, and 2) as much as we agree we are all unique, we often tend to ignore this uniqueness when it comes to perceptions and understanding incoming information. And the way we interpret information has a lot to do with how we react to it, how we think of other people and our relationship with them, and how we expect others to behave. We live and operate in a dynamic, complex, and interconnected world where each one influences everyone else, while there are also millions of other influences at play. The way I react could affect the way people around me react and the other way around. And, the way I react is often a result of the complex interplay of various environmental, cultural, and personal factors. Yet, we expect people to think, perceive and behave in an established stereotypical way. Our friends come over with a grand plan for the weekend, expecting us to be equally hyped about it. Otherwise, we are boring. Our bosses come to us pitching their vision for the team's future or the company and expect us to buy in. Moreover, they don't really want us to speak up unless our view matches theirs, even though they claim to invite varied and even contrasting viewpoints. We are expected to follow certain desirable social norms and etiquette. This is normal to some extent. Otherwise, we will live in an anarchical world, but is it just me thinking that it is increasingly becoming the case these days that the socially acceptable boundaries of behaviour are becoming narrower and that like a Ford Model T, we can be anything we want so long as we are black?

18

Chapter 12 – Attitudes and Attitude Change

"The tough thing about attitudes is that we learn them very early in life. They play a big part in the map of who we are and how we operate."

- Dr. Henry Cloud

Let me ask you a seemingly simple question – what do you think of chocolate? Your opinion could be different from mine, but if I were to answer this question, I would probably say, "It is great, I love chocolate, but I have to be careful with it if I care about my weight and how I look". I assume this could be a popular opinion, but it doesn't matter. What matters is that we have an already formed, off-the-shelf opinion or attitude towards chocolate. We would not start going through everything we know about chocolate from our own experience or from what we have read or heard from others about it. This would be a pretty vexatious and potentially counterproductive task in response to a very simple question. Imagine if we had to perform a complete re-assessment on everything we knew about a person, item, or idea every time one of these questions was brought up in a conversation, or we thought about it.

We have spoken a lot about heuristics and various mental shortcuts that our brains utilise to make information processing more time and energy-efficient in the last few chapters. Forming attitudes about pretty much everything we come across is effectively such a shortcut. Did you know that our brains consume roughly twenty percent of the energy our body uses every day to support its normal functioning[33]? This comes down to twenty percent by an organ, which comprises around only two percent of our weight! And this is the case *after* factoring in many mental shortcuts. If we hadn't developed such mechanisms, the energy consumption levels would have been a lot higher, and we would constantly feel fatigued and unable to do virtually anything else but think.

In this chapter, we will look into personal beliefs and attitudes, and societal pressures to conform to them and try to understand why it is so hard to change them. But, to do that, we need to understand how opinions are formed in the first place. For this chapter, I will use beliefs, opinions, and attitudes interchangeably, because even though there are minor differences in their meanings, they all describe how we feel towards or perceive something.

How Are Beliefs, Opinions, and Attitudes Formed?

There are various ways we form opinions about anything – people, objects, ideas, experiences.

1. Our own experience
2. Observations from others
3. Biologically inherited

We will discuss each of these in turn.

Own Experience

This is probably the most obvious way to form an opinion about something. The process starts from the time we are born. From that point on, life is essentially a never-ending learning process. We put our fingers on the hot stove, burn ourselves, and discover that hot stoves should be avoided (negative attitude). We visit the grandparents, who always buy us ice cream; hence, grandparents are great, and we love them (positive attitude).

Attitudes developed from our own experience tend to be very resilient and resistant to change. This is because we tend to be in love with our perceptions and opinions. How can we not firmly believe something if we saw it or felt it ourselves? So far, so good. But there's just one predicament. We would do well to be mindful to discern the nuances of self-serving, mental shenanigans. This approach makes attitudes very subjective and possibly inconsistent with those of others, which inflates the value of our rightness.

Observations

This is a broad category, encompassing everything from emulating our parents to a wider social circle of relatives, friends, neighbours, and colleagues to country-wide cultural beliefs.

Parents are probably the single most important influence in young individuals' lives and play a decisive role in forming our beliefs and attitudes at a young age. This is hardly surprising. We hear a new word, the meaning of which we don't know, and we immediately run to our parents to ask what it means. Our toy breaks, and we run to our parents to fix it. Our older sibling whoops our ass, and we run to our parents to rat them out. Parents are the panacea for all our problems when we are young, so it is easy to get this perception they are omnipotent and omniscient. Whatever they say and do, must be correct, and our best chance is to follow their lead. Until teenage beckons, that is. During teenage years, we have to do the exact opposite of what they say, of course. But during those initial, formative years of our lives, our parents are our superheroes without capes. Hence, their own views, opinions, and behaviours are critical to shaping the persons we will turn out to be. As we grow up and other people and factors start influencing us, we might end up challenging some of those initial beliefs, but they also tend to be pretty resilient to change. It is amazing how much we still look up to our parents even at a lot more mature stage and use their image/experience/knowledge as a moral compass. If our parents drive an expensive car and value this highly, we are likely to do the same. If our parents got married and had kids at a later age, this also influences our attitude towards marriage and when we feel is appropriate to settle down.

Then, if we look beyond our immediate family, our friends, our teachers, our neighbours, classmates, or colleagues, all play a role in helping to shape our beliefs to some extent. This extent depends on several things, from what they say and if this makes logical sense to who they are, what our opinion of them is, and even something as superficial as how attractive they are. This last part sounds dubious, but if you have stayed with the book (bravo, you're on the right track!), it should not surprise anyone that we are more likely to take advice or believe someone we find attractive or like (not only physically).

A huge part of our adopted opinions and beliefs is attributable to their source. Very often, who is telling us something is just as important as what they are telling us. If this comes from a source of authority or someone we like, we are more than likely to embrace this viewpoint. In social psychology, this is known as evaluative conditioning[34]. We might be sceptical about it, as we would normally think of ourselves as highly logical and intelligent beings who evaluate anything rationally, but if this were true, why would Nike sign a $1 billion worth lifetime contract with the football superstar Cristiano Ronaldo in 2019? To be clear, this is billion with a B. The answer to this is – it was estimated that Cristiano Ronaldo's social media presence generated an estimated $474 million in value for Nike in 2018 alone[35]. It would take just over two years for him to pay off the investment. Yes, Nike is a great brand, and their products are awesome (in my humble opinion), but they know how much exactly it means for them in terms of additional sales to have CR07 show his face wearing their products on TV or a magazine cover. This is almost half a billion of additional sales a year due to us trying to emulate a person we like.

To increase the scale of social observations, we can look at whole national cultures and how these can impact our attitudes. What do you feel about men having more than one wife? If you were born and raised in Europe or North America, where this isn't a common practice, except for some smaller communities, you are likely to exhibit a negative, almost disdainful attitude towards it. It could feel strange, impractical, unnatural, or unequal. If you, however, ask someone born in countries like Algeria, Niger, Saudi Arabia, or Iran, this is not only perfectly acceptable to them. It is the most normal thing in the world because they have spent their lives in an environment where polygamy is rife.

Similarly, if you ask someone how they feel towards immigrants, asylum seekers, and refugees, cultural differences could be between countries or regions. Research suggests that areas that are more ethnically diverse or have a longer history of immigration tend to see this or a lot more favourably, due to their shared history and exposure to immigrants or refugees[36].

This isn't surprising, because as social animals, we shape our opinions to conform to the views of groups with which we most strongly identify. We try to gain acceptance by sharing these views, so the opinions and attitudes of our wider communities also play a big role in the way we shape our outlook of the world.

Heritable

This might come as a surprise, but some of our attitudes are heritable. This goes back to the whole nature versus nurture discussion. It is unclear why some attitudes are more heritable than others, but some research into the topic suggests that this is indeed the case. Some of the most heritable attitudes include those towards abortion, organized religion, reading, or doing athletic activities[37]. All this means is that we are born predisposed to uphold certain beliefs. Simply put, it is in our DNA. If we think about it, this is not entirely surprising. Beliefs and attitudes are a product of our brains, which are passed down to us via DNA from our parents, not unlike anything else like height or body type. This is not to say that these attitudes cannot be altered due to the points we covered earlier e.g., observed behaviour, but we are more predisposed to have them.

One interesting aspect of the heritability of traits has been observed in identical twins. Nancy Segal is one of the researchers who devoted her life to studying twins. In the 1980s and 1990s, she worked on a study of twins separated at birth. She observed remarkable similarities in the personality, intelligence, and beliefs held by identical twins, who had been separated at birth and only met as adults[38]. Having been raised in different families and social circles, personal experience or observed behaviour alone would not explain the striking similarities in their beliefs, which attests to DNA's role in attitude formation.

Why is it so hard to change these beliefs and attitudes?

Have you had an argument with someone, where you keep pulling various logical arguments in favour of your position, and you feel like your opponent's arguments are not nearly as good as yours, but are still unable to drive home your point, much to your chagrin? I have never seen anyone win an argument on a political, religious, or football topic. Bring whatever arguments, statistics, or evidence to the table you want, the other side would not budge. I remember arguing with my dad a few years back over the performance and future of a sports star. It was in light of not very flattering recent performance. My dad argued this was due to them paying a lot more attention to their partner and social media than focusing on sport and how this would cost them otherwise very promising sports future. Meanwhile, I was arguing that social media was a big thing and that everyone else was doing the same, but he wouldn't see it as he wasn't following them (availability bias) and how this sports person's recent performance had nothing to do with social media presence. After about twenty minutes of a very heated debate, we achieved nothing but ruining dinner for everyone else and not talking for a few days after that, thanks to our mutual intransigence. Any of that sounds familiar? Here are a few reasons for this.

Emotional investment and association

The problem with changing one's beliefs or attitudes is that we do not argue against one specific point here and now, we argue against years of accrued beliefs, individuals, and experiences, which have led to the formation of these attitudes. This could do with some explanation, and yes, you guessed it right, examples.

Example 1: I have always believed in education and its myriad benefits on future career prospects. The logic goes something like that: if I want to have a good and comfortable life, I need to find a good and lucrative job. This, in turn, requires a solid academic foundation. I wasn't born with this belief; I mainly adopted it from my parents. Both of my parents are quite ambitious people and were pushing both my sister and me to excel academically. This isn't just my parents though, a lot of people generally believe that education, while no guarantee or an absolute requirement for success, is an important contributing factor. Having been raised with this sentiment, I have spent the vast majority of my life studying diligently to get top grades at school, at university, and later in pursuing various professional qualifications. The result is that, while I now fully appreciate there are plenty of examples of very successful people who do not have a university or even a high school degree, and that various paths do pave the way for success, with education being just one of them, I would argue to death about its merits. And this is because, if you decide to argue with me against it, you will not be arguing with me here and now. Instead, you will be arguing with what my parents believed, what many other people around me believed, and more importantly, with twenty-five years of effort, sweat, and hopes, which I have invested in this belief. This attitude has become a part of me, and accepting this as wrong would mean throwing twenty-five years of hard work under the bus. It is too big an investment to dismiss lightly.

Example 2: Cultural beliefs and attitudes towards abortion. This is one of the topics with marked cultural differences in opinion. It is not my intention to argue for or against in this book, but I just wanted to highlight the stark gap we have in abortion attitudes between countries and cultures. A study done way back in 2005 on how people across ten European countries felt towards women who were given the right to abortion indicated an average of 63% approval rating[39]. Some of the countries in this research included Czech Republic, Finland, France, Germany, Italy, and the UK. In comparison, another research measuring similar attitudes in countries with strong Christian influence like Brazil, Chile, and the Philippines, measured around 23% approval[40]. (Note: these were two separate pieces of research and there could be differences in calculation methodologies employed, but the contrast is too stark to be disregarded). This demonstrates that religion plays a large part in this argument due to the involvement of concepts like moral rectitude and, consequently, one's eternal future. It could be hard to convince a devout Christian of one's right to abortion, especially as religious beliefs are particularly hard to alter (ignoring some more liberal strains of the religion).

Example 3: Many people have idols, be it a sports star like Serena Williams, a popular actor like Brad Pitt, or a technocrat like Elon Musk. We tend to identify closely with the views espoused by our idols and have a more positive attitude towards something only because we associate it with them. This is the evaluative conditioning point I had touched upon some time back. And then, we have the halo effect, according to which we feel positively towards a person in a given aspect, only because we like them in another aspect. Succinctly put, these two effects imply that we would tend to agree with and see something more favourably if it comes from someone we like, even if they are far from being subject matter experts (which is a worrying fact, but that's the way we are). So, assume you have someone like Eva Longoria, who goes on TV and talks about recycling and environmentally sustainable living. She might not be an ecologist or, in any capacity expert in the field, but if you like her as an actress, you will be a lot more receptive to the ideas she communicates about green/environmentally-friendly living. Here, the strength of the attitude comes from how strongly we identify with her and see her as someone to emulate. So, trying to argue against this would effectively mean going against our idol.

The above examples demonstrate our proclivity to get emotionally invested in ideas and attitudes, not necessarily due to their logical grounds, but rather due to the power of association or high personal investment, making them particularly challenging to alter.

Consistent sense of self (self-affirmation)

Most people hold a positive view of themselves. We covered this at length in previous chapters, so I will spare you the details here, but the self-affirmation theory[41] effectively posits that we are motivated to maintain beliefs, which protect a positive view of ourselves. This would also mean that we are more resistant to change of attitudes which jeopardise our sense of self. Thus, this is also related to cognitive dissonance reduction, something that this book has already covered. Let's assume Person X is not a particularly environmentally cautious person. They don't often recycle. If ever, they always take the car to go to the shop, even if this is to save them a five-minute walk, and they buy a new plastic bag every time they shop, as opposed to carrying a reusable one from home. This is because recycling wasn't a big thing when Person X was growing up, and they have not been raised with a very eco-focused mindset. Now, assume Person Y comes over and advocates the benefits of recycling and living more sustainably. Person X initially dismisses it as something they don't really care about. But then Person Y, a fervent environmentalist, gets agitated by their message not getting through and raises the tone, throwing some more aggressive comments, which Person X can no longer ignore. Now they feel under direct attack and are ready to fight back. This is because their sense of self and what they stand for is challenged. The likely outcome of this is Person X, closing their mind down and refuting every argument made by Person Y, even if it is a perfectly valid one.

To this, we can also add the social cost of changing views. It is not only a question of how we see ourselves but also how others see us. Have you ever ardently defended a view in the past, only to have your stance changed, whether as a result of new experiences, additional evidence coming to light, or some other reason? How likely are you to argue against your previous view? Possibly not very, as you want to avoid the perceived shame of effectively acknowledging you were wrong back then. Of course, the mature thing to do is concede you were wrong, but God, we detest the "I told you so".

Failure to register conflicting opinions

A more recent piece of research, performed by a team of researchers from City University, University College London, and the Museum of Science and Industry in Chicago, has come up with some intriguing findings. The research team attempted to determine why it is so hard to change people's opinions and attitudes by looking into what happens in the brain using MRI scans. In this experiment, volunteers were recruited and randomly paired in couples. Each volunteer was then presented properties they had to value and suggest how much they would be willing to invest. Once all properties were valued, each couple was placed in a twinned scanner to monitor their brain activity. After that, they were once again shown the properties and their estimates as a reminder, followed by the estimates of their partners. When focusing on the posterior medial prefrontal cortex, the part of the brain involved in evaluating someone else's ideas, brain activity was recorded when the other person's estimate matched the subject's i.e. when they agreed. However, then there was a disagreement: that part of the brain failed to record any change in brain activity. The scientists concluded that participants just failed to record the conflicting argument[42]. This is, of course, just one research and like everything else, the results should be viewed with a healthy dose of scepticism, but this would imbue a lot of clarity about the difficulty we experience when it comes to changing our beliefs.

What does all that mean in today's context?

A very good question. I have written all of the above as a preface of sorts, leading up to the real focus of this chapter – social pressures and society-wide mind-set shifts. We all live in a world where we tend to (or are impelled to) do a lot more thinking than ever before. We have moved away from meeting our most basic needs to a much more elevated stage, where everyone hypothesises about the world, what this world should look like, and how it has to change. I believe, like in many other aspects, the world has culturally changed a lot more in the last twenty-thirty years than for centuries before that. I would even argue, this change has come way too fast for us to keep up emotionally with it. It is possibly due to the power of technology and mass media, possibly because we do not have to worry about famine, war, or survival as much as any other time before this, or likely due to a combination of factors, but today, we focus a lot more on what makes us happy, what we want to do, or who we want to become. Life has never been easier and more convenient, and our biological needs are over-satisfied, which is why we can afford to ruminate on some of the wider questions about life, society, and idealism. This considerably more comfortable life has made us soft compared to previous generations, and we are terrified of having our feelings hurt. We are more than happy to go on social media and rant about anything and anyone that even slightly upsets us as if life is meant to be perfect and we are meant to be in a constant state of happiness.

We constantly judge people for saying this or doing that, which even remotely hurts our own beliefs and perceptions. But where we fail is in the understanding that everyone else is merely the product of their environment. If Person A could somehow walk in Person B's shoes, share every experience, every contact, and every influence, Person B has been subjected to, the likelihood is that Person A should have very similar views and beliefs. We should not hate, attack, or ostracise people for holding beliefs different from ours, because they were the product of subjective experiences and influences. This is not to suggest that we must always shun any disagreement with others. All I am saying is that we cannot judge them for having a different belief from our own, even if this belief is wrong in our own eyes.

These days, there are large-scale movements are causing social upheavals towards perceptions of women, minorities, and various freedom movements. Many of these are undoubtedly long overdue. These aim to sever ties with long-established stigmas and promote a freer, less judgmental, and more liberal society. These are all noble objectives. However, they are, by no means, easy or quick to attain. Achieving a large-scale paradigm shift would take decades to take hold. While we have the technology to reach people around the globe instantaneously, no technology can change people's minds overnight. If you have learned anything from this chapter so far, it is this: you are going to find it extremely difficult to alter beliefs, which have been built over many years before that.

Paradoxically, instead of becoming freer, our society becomes more judgmental than ever before. We expect people to appreciate our uniqueness, but we fail to appreciate theirs. We expect people to get over their subjective experiences, contacts, and pre-held beliefs, even their biological programming, which make them unique and adopt modern views in the blink of an eye and shame those who do not. We are not computers whose memory could be wiped clean and start fresh. Achieving a large-scale social shift is an onerous, painstaking process that has already started and I believe is very much irreversible, and for the better. As humans, we are exceptional beings, capable of a lot, but Rome wasn't built in a day.

19

Chapter 13 – Willpower

"Each January 1, millions of people drag themselves out of bed, full of hope or hangover, resolved to eat less, exercise more, spend less money, work harder at the office, keep the home cleaner, and still miraculously have more time for romantic dinners and long walks on the beach. By February 1, they're embarrassed to even look at the list."

- Roy F. Baumeister

Let's talk about New Year's resolutions. Do you make any? A lot of people do. What will I change for the better or achieve more this year? It is a good idea, I guess. If New Year's resolutions give you a bit of extra motivation to make a positive change, then why not do it? We should always strive to do better or be a better version of ourselves. I do believe that. Yet, I have stopped making resolutions for two reasons: One – I don't think one should wait for a specific day in the year to introduce a positive change to their life. You want to change something for the better – start now, regardless of what day it is; and two - I have discovered that I am terrible at following through and that making any resolutions is just an irredeemable loss of five precious minutes of my life. I have been getting abs every year for the last ten years. I still don't have any. Thank God that most women don't even like abs. This is what my fiancé keeps telling me anyway. Isn't she super sweet?

People's goals would be different even though some typical ramblings can indeed be found: This year I will tone up… I will quit smoking… I will spend more time with my family… I will get a better job, etc. But regardless of what they are, there is usually a big trade-off – ambition versus willingness to follow through and make the required sacrifices, whether it is time, money, effort, or something else. Oh, if only one could have a body like Dwayne Johnson while sitting on the couch and eating pizza.

The sad truth of life is that nothing good comes easily. Hard work, dedication, and sweat are just part of the price we have to pay to get from where we are now to where we want to be. But what is the one thing that makes us tick and keep pushing us to make these sacrifices? The simple answer is – WILLPOWER! The not so simple part is – willpower is hard to muster, it is finite, and mine specifically depletes pretty quickly.

The benefits of having strong willpower are undeniable and even measurable. It keeps complacency at bay and propels us to accomplish our goals, whether it is healthier, wealthier, or a better version of ourselves in any shape or form. It makes us spend time working on a personal project, choose a salad over a burger, resist the chocolate bar in the supermarket, stay away from the casino or put down a cigarette. People frequently report a lack of willpower as the biggest deterrent to change. And on the other side, various studies conclude that people with stronger willpower are not only happier, healthier, and better at managing stress but are also able to form stronger relationships, and are generally more successful in life[43]. But the nice and easy part ends here. Mustering enough willpower to act is a completely different ball game. Sometimes you have it, and sometimes you don't. You love it when you do and try to do the most while it lasts, and then wait for the next fortuitous moment when it returns. Something like your salary – it comes, you are living life for a few days until it is over, and then eagerly await the next one. Yes, I hear you. This is the story of 95% of the people's lives. But, to understand more about its ephemeral nature, we need to dig a little deeper, starting with the brain's structure. Don't worry, I will keep it high level.

The structure of the human brain is incredibly complex with different parts being responsible for specific functions. However, we often think of our brains as having two main parts, which control our thought process and emotions – the prefrontal cortex, all smart, rational, and disciplined, trying to push us towards doing the right thing; and the amygdala, the more emotional and irrational part (in reality, the amygdala is a tiny part of our brain, but disproportionately powerful when it comes to influencing our decisions). Unsurprisingly, willpower, which pushes us to resist temptation, stay strong, and do the right thing, resides in the prefrontal cortex. Interestingly, while the overall size of the human brain has tripled in size as part of our evolution, the increase in the size of the prefrontal cortex alone has been six times[43]. From an evolutionary perspective, the importance of this part of the brain has increased as we turned into Homo sapiens. Studies also show that his part of the brain is also the last one to attain maturation with its development not complete until around the age of 25[43]. This explains a lot about those high school and university years, doesn't it!

Being the grown-up in this symbiotic relationship, the prefrontal cortex needs to fend off the amygdala and control its behaviour all the time, but that requires much effort. So, the more controlling and resisting it has to do, the more energy it burns until it can no longer fight. Think about the two as a parent and a young child. The child (amygdala) does nothing but run around, scream, and throw its toys out of the pram any time it wants something, and it doesn't care about doing the right things. It is all about, I want, what I want, when I want. On the other hand, the prefrontal cortex is the parent who constantly needs to look after the child, control its behaviour, and make sure it doesn't eat dirt off the ground, run in front of a car, or draw all over the wallpapers. And like every parent, the prefrontal cortex is absolutely shattered at the end of the day and just acquiesces.

All of this implies that willpower is not a renewable source of energy in that it is not limitless. The more we use it throughout the day, the less is left to control our behaviour and push us towards making the right decision. In psychology parlance, this effect is known as ego depletion[44]. Scientists explain this effect with glucose levels in the brain, which is the fuel our brain consumes to stay active and self-regulate our behaviour. As we make decisions or choices throughout the day, these glucose levels inevitably get depleted. Every day, we make thousands of decisions, whether consciously or unconsciously, from solving a specific problem at work or personal life through trivial ones like what to wear or what to grab for lunch to unconscious ones that we do not even register. One source suggests we make staggering 35,000 decisions every day[45]. We may not realise it, but each of these burns a small amount of glucose in our brains, thereby curtailing our latent potential to resist temptation later. Having said that, it is hardly surprising that many people recommend building some sort of a daily routine as a willpower-boosting mechanism because this reduces the number of choices we get to make. This is not new, and you might be surprised to find out that many famous and successful people have adopted this approach. Mark Zuckerberg, Steve Jobs, Albert Einstein, Barack Obama are/were just some of the people known to wear the same clothes all the time for one simple reason – reduce the number of decisions made daily, thus boosting their mental capabilities.

We cannot talk about ego depletion without mentioning one of the key contributors to this theory - the American social psychologist Roy Baumeister, who performed the now popular chocolate and radish experiment back in 1996[46]. The experiment was simple. Baumeister and his colleagues recruited participants and split them into two groups. Participants in group one were put in a room where freshly baked chocolate cookies were on display, and participants were allowed to eat them. Participants in the second group were presented with cookies and radish. However, they were not allowed to touch the cookies, so they had to sit there for a few minutes and resist the temptation. The real experiment commenced after that. All participants were asked to solve a puzzle. The puzzle was unsolvable, but they didn't know that at the time. The scientists observed that, on average, group two gave up twice as fast as group one. This was a demonstration of depleted willpower i.e., the mental strength required to resist those cookies then impaired the participants' persistence and willingness to tackle the hard challenge.

Multiple subsequent experiments have demonstrated this effect. It will be unfair, however, to bypass some worthwhile criticism of this theory. Life would be just too simple if everyone agreed on the same thing, wouldn't it? Some studies tell us that willpower does not work like a muscle and hence, it doesn't wear down; instead, it is in unlimited supply. Proponents of this view opine that even thinking of will-power as being limited is not devoid of dangers as this would deter us from doing the hard thing – in the sense of making excuses like "I can't do X because I have worked very hard today, and my willpower is depleted" kind of thing.

Despite this criticism, I think the ego-depletion theory has a certain appeal (you do not have to agree with me). It resonates well with me, as I can find a lot of my behaviour conforming to the model. I find it a lot easier to stay strong and do the right thing on the weekend or after a good day at work (I define a good day at work as one where I have finished more or less on time and not had to deal with a thousand problems). If I have had a good day at work, it is easier for me to have a salad in the evening or engage in productive behaviours like working on my projects. This smooth sailing has allowed me to reduce the ego mentioned above depletion and made it easier to resist a naughty meal in the evening. Now, consider a contrasting example for a moment – you have had a terrible day, where everything that could go wrong has gone wrong, and you have been fighting fires all day. You are mentally drained at the end of the day, and you want to grab some food. How likely are you to have a naughty meal or pour yourself a drink, thinking, "f*** it, I deserve this"? It cannot be just me doing that, right? Come on, I trust you to be honest on this issue! Coming back to the larger point I am trying to make. It doesn't really matter if it is indulging in unhealthy food, drinking, snapping at your partner, smoking, or just watching TV instead of doing something more productive. You know it is bad. You know you will regret it tomorrow or in the longer term, but you just couldn't care less right now.

If we think about willpower as a finite resource or as a muscle that can be strengthened to endure more, just like any other muscle in our body, then the million-dollar question is – HOW? How do I increase my mental capacity to resist temptation and stay in control? There are lots of strategies that different people suggest. I will list some of the key ones, but my intention is not to explore them in detail. You can google a zillion articles on the topic.

1. Get enough good quality sleep – research suggests that insufficient sleep (under at least six hours) deters the behaviour controlling ability of the pre-frontal cortex over the amygdala. Put simply, sleep deprivation makes us less likely to be successful in resist temptation. In more extreme scenarios, one research conducted over alcohol and drug abusers shows that getting enough sleep makes people less likely to lapse[47].
2. Plan ahead and introduce a routine – I briefly touched on this point earlier. If decisions and choices drain our mental energy, planning ahead or following a routine, which brings down the number of decisions we need to make, helps reduce the energy drain. This can mean anything from making a meal plan for the week to scheduling activities in your diary; the idea is to make fewer choices, which is bound to do a world of good to your most trusted alibi – your mental strength.

3. Avoid temptation and distraction – if you have a sweet tooth, do not buy lots of chocolate and sweets to store in the cupboard or leave them lying around on the exhibit. It is quite self- explanatory, really. It is hard to resist sweets, a drink, cigarettes, or whatever your vice is, when it is, in your face all the time. Every time you look at it, you get a step closer to failing to control yourself. You do not need superhuman strength to resist it, just a bit of smart planning and common sense.
4. Start small and introduce a reward system – life-changing decisions rarely happen overnight, so start small. Introduce interim goals, and work towards your objectives one step at a time. Reward yourself with a little treat only after you have reached a milestone.
5. Set realistic goals and work on one thing at a time – we often fail because we set unrealistic objectives or expectations. So, when we fail to meet these objectives fast enough, we grow frustrated and just give up. Like I said before, positive change will not happen overnight. And do not try to do everything at the same time—those New Year's resolutions, for example. If you made five of them, don't try and hit all five at the time. Focus on one, get it done, and move on to the next one.

There are a lot more practices and tips available out there, but I will stop here because, otherwise, I will start sounding way too positive and can easily be mistaken for one of those self-proclaimed self-help gurus who preach the "if you can imagine it, you can do it" kind of bulls***. Don't get me wrong; I am a big believer in self-improvement, doing the right thing, and always trying to be a better version of ourselves. But also true to myself and the general tone of this book, we do not live in an ideal world where we can achieve anything we set our minds on. There are way too many variables, way too many limitations, way too many externalities that stymie our potential for success. We can sit here, planning our meals for the week, reading aspirational quotes about how the sky is the limit, drawing diagrams of how to get from point A (where we are now) to point B (where we want to be), and so on, but then life happens, and shit hits the roof. You go to work, and trouble greets you from the moment you walk through the door, making you come face-to-face with an endless string of issues and escalations. And then, someone brings doughnuts and leaves them next to you. Or you are trying to do a few things at once – cooking food, listening to your best friend complaining how their life couldn't get any more miserable, minding your new-born, and trying to get to the door to accept a delivery. At the same time, your 3-year-old has found your wallet and is practising its scissor cutting skills. Or you have spent ten hours juggling work, domestic chores, and homeschooling your kids. After a hellish day like that, good luck finding the motivation in you to reach the sky. You are sitting there thinking about how you can put off your mini project to the weekend. But then the weekend comes, and after the hell of a week you have had, dragging yourself out of bed only to move to the couch and put the TV on is as much willpower you could muster because you are as lifeless as you can be. There is, of course, next week, next month, or a far more realistic possibility - never.

Thankfully, life is neither constantly bad nor constantly good; it ebbs and flows. Sometimes we feel energized, happy, relaxed, and a lot more able to get hold of our lives. Other times, it is just bad. The most important thing we can do is realise this dual nature of our existence and accept it. Don't beat yourself up for failing to adhere to your routine, getting a bit out of shape, falling behind schedule occasionally, or wasting some time in utterly useless non-value-added activity if it helps you relax. No one's life is perfect, and we all have our share of good and bad moments. On this note, I want to conclude this chapter with some interesting facts about the effects of feeling guilty and beating yourself up when you have had a willpower failure. Popular belief is that letting yourself off the hook, once you have lapsed, accelerates the pathway to failures because it essentially gives you a free pass to do it again by not taking responsibility. This might come as a surprise, but various pieces of research suggest the exact opposite. For example, one experiment in 2007 asked dieters to have a doughnut. After this initial willpower failure, they were given a range of candies and asked to evaluate them, explaining that they could eat as much candy as they needed to assess them. Of course, the real objective of the test was not to evaluate candies but to assess how much each individual would eat after the initial failure with the doughnut. One significant distinction deserves mention here. After eating the doughnut, some participants were given a pep talk about how it was okay that they had it, how it happens to everyone, and how they should not beat themselves due to guilt. This was intended to reduce the feeling of guilt and shame experienced by them. According to the findings, people who were given this guilt-relieving message ate less than half of the candy than those who weren't told anything[48].

The same effect was demonstrated by looking into drinking, gambling, and procrastinating. This is because feeling a strong sense of remorse after a failure makes you search for comfort, which often is the exact same thing you have been trying to avoid in the first place. This feeling of guilt and shame puts us into a mindset that is a lot more susceptible to anxiety and makes us crave instant gratification[49]. This is the exact opposite of the mindset required to channel your willpower and push you towards that better version of yourself.

So, next time your willpower lapses, don't judge yourself too hard and remember these key things:

1. You are not perfect, and you will never be, but neither is anyone else
2. It happens to everyone
3. There are several things you can do to give yourself a better chance next time
4. You cannot control everything in life, and sometimes, our failures are outside of our control
5. And most importantly – you are only human.

20

Chapter 14 – Failure and Blame

> *"Success is stumbling from failure to failure with no loss of enthusiasm."*
> - Winston Churchill

The previous chapter looked into willpower failures, i.e., foregoing long-term benefits for short-term pleasure/gains, and how ego depletion influences this. In this chapter, I would like to discuss failure in general and our attitude towards it. This is vital because we have a complex relationship with failure, often giving rise to feelings of sadness, anger, guilt, and a vicious cycle of blame-game. This has a longer-term impact on our confidence and prospects, as we all have relationships with others.

One of my all-time-favourite quotes is "success has many fathers, but failure is an orphan." The quote's origin is undetermined, some attribute it to John F Kennedy, others to the Roman historian Tacitus, who lived millennia ago, but that is not the point. This powerful quote requires little explanation and is way too common in life. There is a very simple explanation for this – we are terrified of failure. We hate it and often beat ourselves up when it happens. In my opinion, this is because 1) – it hurts our ego, and 2) – it causes us to feel shameful in front of others. Let's look into each one of these in turn.

The ego factor - we discussed the role of ego at length earlier in the book. Simply put, our sense of self-worth gets inflated by successes and deflated by failures. We all have some view of our own worth, which, in many cases, is slightly inflated because it helps us to feel good about ourselves. Every success reinforces this view; it flatters the ego and keeps it happy. On the other side, failure is a sobering realisation that we are not flawless or impervious to failures. And, while our rational brains already know this, the ego is a slow learner. It sort of knows the truth but doesn't want to accept it.

The shame factor – unlike the ego, shame has an external expression. It reflects how others see us and feel about us. In this respect, fear of failure is nothing more than fear that others might think less of us. I know many people would say: "I don't care what others think of me". Sorry if I sound a bit harsh, but that is utter nonsense! Everyone does, it's just that some people don't want to admit it because they dread the prospect of being rejected. The "you can't hurt me if I don't care what you think" kind of thing is nothing more than a defence mechanism. Be that as it may, the fear of shame is quite real. I believe that the best way to judge if this is a factor for you is to ask yourself: "Would I care about failing if no one else knew?" or "Would I be more likely to take a risk and possibly fail if I were the only one who would know?"

Both of these points underscore a deeper problem with failure – our attitude towards it. It only makes us feel ashamed, because we have an unhealthy attitude to it. We often see it as a degrading, utter expression of incompetence, the worst possible thing ever. Some of this is cultural, some of it we adopt from our parents, and some of it is imbibed in our organisations' cultures. It wouldn't take a rocket scientist to figure out that parents are probably the single most important factor because of the huge influence over us when building up our character and our worldviews in our formative years. I could also add school teachers to this category. How did you feel when you got a bad grade at school, failed an exam, or weren't selected for the school's football/hockey/basketball team? More importantly, how did your parents or teachers make you feel? Did you get a pep talk like "Listen, it is not a big deal, it happens, you will do better next time" or "You are embarrassing yourself and us. You have to be ashamed of yourself". Similarly, did you see your parents failing shortly after starting a business and taking it on the chin, or were they blaming themselves and others, creating a disconcerting atmosphere of gloom and doom? These early experiences are vital for shaping our attitudes in life. Similarly, the organisational culture and the manner in which it handles mistakes is also critical to our perceptions. Every organisation should strive to minimize failures, which could have reputational, operational, or financial repercussions. But does your organisation see mistakes as learning opportunities or a convenient opportunity to name and shame those it couldn't care less about? The latter is not conducive to promulgating autonomy or creativity, which are so important for success. In my professional experience, I have seen both, and it has a massive impact on one's attitude towards the company itself. Such firms tend to have higher attrition rates and lower loyalty in the workplace.

It is completely natural to feel disappointment when we make a mistake, or when something does not go our way. We have invested effort, time, hopes, sometimes money, and resources, and seeing all of this go down the drain is not a nice feeling. There is nothing illogical or unnatural about this. I would even argue, this is essential. If we did not care about the outcome, why do it in the first place? Why would we try and learn from this failure and improve in the future? But, on the other hand, feeling a lingering sense of guilt or remorse is unlikely to get us anywhere. All it will do is create psychological strain and prevent us from trying again next time. Because why would you do it all again if the outcome of another potential failure is so severe? Maybe it is better to just leave it there and accept it will never happen. By doing so, we will not be moving forward, but at least we won't be facing another energy-sapping episode of self-pity and despondence. This is the kind of thinking, which will have you stuck in your comfort zone (make that mediocrity), and never moving forward because failure is an indelible part of success. From this perspective, moving on with our lives requires a paradigm shift, a complete revamp of the way we perceive failure.

Failure is an integral part of life

There is no scenario in this world where we would always succeed or win. Success and failure are functions of time, effort, knowledge, planning, luck, various externalities, etc. None of us can process all information to consider every eventuality, pre-empting and mitigating all known and unknown risks, or controlling all factors at play. If there exists such a person, I am yet to meet him. Yes, preparation and planning are often vital for success, but they do not guarantee success at all times. Consider the following examples:

1. You have planned the trip of your life to an exotic country for your big 30th, 40th, or 50th birthday. You have various maps, time schedules, activities, everything planned out to the smallest detail. However, one week before you are due to go, a global pandemic erupts, and all travel is banned. You have done all you can, but you are still dependent on various externalities, which are way beyond your control.
2. You are a professional tennis player. You have qualified for your first big tournament; this is your chance to shine and make the breakthrough of your life. You have

trained tirelessly for months for this tournament, let alone the years of practice you have had to get to this point. You have researched your opponents, performed the mental visualisation and physical exercises that are supposed to be done, and left no stone unturned. The big day comes, but you draw one of the top three contenders in the competition and lose. There is no drama here, no blame, nothing you could have done better. You put all the required effort, but your opponent was simply better than you. And you've got to accept defeat unless you are the best person in the world in your field. There will always be someone better than you on a given day. All we can do is fail, learn, and try to do better next time.

3. You are working on a large-scale project at a large corporate behemoth that includes hundreds of people globally. Anyone who has been associated with a monster of a project such as this would concur that there are so many links in the chain and so many interdependencies that it is impossible to plan, consider and assess everything. There will always be unknowns and problems popping up out of the blue. Here is a curious fact about WW II to illustrate this point. During the German attack of Stalingrad during WW II, when the Germans started losing the battle, they desperately sought reinforcements. Twenty-second Panzer tank division was sitting in reserve, ready to be called into battle… except they weren't quite ready when the time came. Out of the

104 tanks, 62 weren't running properly or would not start at all. The issue – field mice! During the period of inactivity, field mice had nested inside the tanks and eaten the insulation of the wiring systems[50]. Out of all the possible problems, one could worry about when at war, who could have thought about field mice eating the wiring of the tanks?

There are just a few examples, but you get the point. There are days when you need to accept reality, be honest with yourself about what transpired, and what you can do to make things better going forward.

Everybody fails

Oftentimes we look at famous people whom we consider successful, smiling on camera, or on the cover of a magazine, and think they have it all. Maybe they do, maybe they don't. I strongly believe no one has it all, success in one aspect of life often comes at the expense of another, but that's not what I would like you to focus on. They seem to have it all and be on top of the world in their respective fields. This is wonderful for them, but what we see is just the tip of the iceberg. We do not see all the efforts, hardship, and failed attempts they have gone through to get to this point. This reminds me of another one of my favourite quotes – "Success is like being pregnant. Everyone says Congratulations, but nobody knows how many times you were f***ed". Anyone who has ever made it anywhere can attest to this and tell you how often they have been f***ed.

Bill Gates is a poignant case in point. As one of the wealthiest people in the world, he can certainly qualify as a success story on the entrepreneurial scene. But he wasn't born a billionaire and certainly not immune to failures. His first venture, Traf-o-Data, established with partners in 1972, to read raw data from traffic counters and give information to traffic engineers, struggled for a few years, and eventually closed shop. This, however, didn't discourage him or his ambitions. He went on to establish Microsoft, and the rest is history. And just to be clear, while Microsoft has become an enormous success and one of the most respected companies in the world, that doesn't mean Gates succeeded every step of the way. There have been many failures along the way, including failing to build the world's leading search engine in competition with Google, which as Gates admitted in an interview years later, kicked his ass.

Similarly, James Dyson, the billionaire inventor of the famous Dyson vacuum cleaners, had to create 5127 vacuum prototypes before he eventually got the design right[51]. Can you imagine the resilience and drive this man had to keep going after over FIVE THOUSAND failed attempts? There are many more examples, including Henry Ford, Steve Jobs, and Richard Branson as some of the most high-profile ones. So, if you want some motivation to keep trying, look no further than these luminaries who failed and failed consistently until they attained some semblance of success.

Failure as a function of risk and the risk-return relationship

We cannot discuss failure, without mentioning risk and return. One of the most pervasive relationships governing the world is that between risk and reward. The higher the risk (and by extension probability of failure), the higher the potential reward. Some people are very risk-averse and more than happy to stay where they are, sticking to the status quo without taking too much risk. This is unlikely to lead to big gains, but not everyone is after these big gains. Conversely, if you want to make it big, you will need to take a certain amount of risk, and be very mindful that you could also lose big.

Failure as a learning opportunity and a stepping stone

They say, "The only real mistake is the one you learn nothing from". If failure is inevitable from time to time, the best thing we can do is learn from it. But to do that, we need to start with a mindset, which is conducive to it i.e., accept the failure. Learning cannot start if we don't acknowledge that something needs to be learned. A fearful attitude towards failure can stifle the process either by suppressing the thought that a failure happened, externalising it (i.e., attributing it to an external factor) or blame-shifting (blaming someone else). Once we accept and make peace with a setback, we give ourselves a good chance to start learning and by extension, healing.

There are few failures in life we cannot recover from

Lastly, we are a resilient species. However bad the problem, mistake or failure is, there is little that is beyond repair. There are, of course, failures that are very costly, for instance, not adhering to the correct medical procedures leading to a loss of life, plane crashes, or mistakes in industrial plants, which could cost multiple lives or invite large-scale catastrophes. While impactful, we shouldn't forget that doctors, pilots, and industrial workers are humans and not failure-proof. Luckily, not every failure has or can have fatal consequences, and most of our failures can seem trivial in comparison and little that we cannot recover from. Every time something doesn't go my way, I ask myself, "So what? What is the implication?" Then I try to focus on the positives in my life and the fact that whatever has happened shall pass. There is no point losing sleep over it. I know it sounds flippant and disingenuous, but statements like "it is only work" or "it is only money" do help.

As I am writing all this, I do still wonder, "Does any of this help?" The thing about failure is that, like any other feeling, it has an emotional expression. It invokes feelings of sadness, disappointment, shame, guilt, etc. The problem with feelings is – they are incompatible with reasoning. It doesn't matter how many logical arguments I can pull to argue that it is pointless to feel a certain way. This will never change so long as we perceive failure as something grotesque or tragic. The very act of failing our driving test doesn't make us sad. It makes us sad because we think of it as something bad. It is only by changing this perception of failure as something negative, that we get rid of unwanted emotions. However, going through such a complete emotional transformation would be a major feat even for the most devoted stoic.

I cannot imagine a human being, who would not feel at least a bit of disappointment or sadness from a failure. But hopefully, the above points would help reduce the emotional strain and catalyse the healing process by appreciating that failure is sure to happen from time to time, that it happens to everyone, and that it can be used as a stepping stone for future successes. I will conclude with the famous quote by Thomas Edison whom a reporter asked about how it felt to fail a thousand times until he invented the light bulb. Edison responded: "I didn't fail a thousand times. The light bulb was an invention with a thousand steps"[52].

21

Chapter 15 – Social Comparisons

"The reason we struggle with insecurity is because we compare our behind the scenes with everyone else's highlight reel."
- Steve Furtick

I am a big believer in competition. I believe that competition is the key driving force behind humankind's evolution to where we are now. In fact, survival of the fittest is quite literally a life and death competition itself. We ended up 'conquering' land, sea, air…and more recently outer space because someone wanted to achieve more, to do more, to win more. It is that visceral human drive to outdo ourselves or the rest that allowed us to build higher, travel faster, and top every other achievement of the past. Imagine living in a world where you would sail for months to get from Europe to the Americas instead of taking a few-hour flight. This was the reality not so long ago but inconceivable from the viewpoint of a modern person in the 21st century. None of what we take for granted nowadays would be possible if someone thought they were happy with what they had and hadn't challenged the status quo.

However, there are two sides to competition as well. One that isn't prompted by self-improvement, but by self-enhancement i.e., making ourselves feel better. We tend to compare ourselves to others in a constant race at who has a better car, a bigger TV, who earns more, or whose kids have done better at school. This is so typical, especially for the western individualist societies, where we attach more importance to individual accomplishments than collective achievements. We identify with our belongings and "successes". The latest model smartphone or a flashy car flaunts our affluence and status. Having a bigger lawn than our neighbour is a 'clear testament' to our superiority. Earning more than our colleagues proves that we are better than them. These are important to us because they feed our ego, and we already know how much we care about them. It is a living thing, which must be fed with new belongings and pseudo achievements.

None of this is new. In many ancient states and empires, societal status was measured by gold, land, or the number of slaves one had. Not too dissimilar to today, except that slaves are definitely not cool in the 21st century. We have servants or employees instead. The point is, showcasing wealth and achievements to make us look better than others is not a recent phenomenon. However, the advancement of technology, the internet, and social media has catapulted this to a whole different level. It was easy back in the pre-Facebook and Instagram days. When I was a kid in the 90s, there were only about ten kids on the block I played with, a few more at my school to whom I was close enough to know what they were up to. That was it. I competed with twenty kids for the title of "best footballer", having a better PC", "having the coolest trainers", etc. These days, you have to compete with the whole world. We have hundreds or thousands of social media friends, contacts, or followers globally. Keeping up with all of them is tough. There will always be someone younger, richer, better, more successful than we are. Especially so when everyone is in the business of faking happiness. You throw the marketers and credit cards in the mix, and you get a perfect vanity storm.

Start with the marketers. It is a vast industry worth $1.7 trillion as per a 2019 study[53], which mainly exists to convince us that we need something, which we don't, or that we need something to express our identity. Go get this new pair of trainers which can be personalised to match your colourful personality. Buy this new watch because it is a true fit for a successful person like you. Rent this office in the city centre and demonstrate to your clients that you are a successful and credible brand. Hundreds of ads scream at us daily, trying to convince us what we need something else to be special, remarkable, and unique. It is almost as if the worst thing we can be today is average, just a man or a woman among eight billion others in this world.

Then, we have an ostensible untameable beast called social media, where everyone is constantly happy and the best versions they could be. How often do we see posts or pictures chronicling someone's everyday life, struggles, or failures? The vast majority of posts try to convince us how happy and successful everyone else is. Jenny got promoted because she is incredible at what she does. Mark went on an incredible holiday to Bali and posted fifty pictures of beautiful scenery and big smiles. Theo just bought a second expensive car because owning one does a great deal of disservice to his reputation. Claire just got engaged, and look at the size of this rock! Even a 'regular morning coffee' picture is anything but regular. You clean your otherwise dirty table, pour your coffee in your special cup, maybe brush the dust off some book and place it in the background as it will give you this sophisticated look. You then spend the next 5-10 minutes trying to take the perfect shot from the best angle. Voila! Here is your 'regular morning coffee' shot. Lastly, make sure you post in on social media, because what is the point of all this if no one sees it... #justmyregularcoffeeshot. Everyone is doing their best to prove that they are happy, successful, and essentially better than us. All this does is leaving us upset, feeling a bit inferior, dissatisfied with ourselves. Everyone is having a great time, but us. So, we return the 'virtual favour'. We don't like being left behind (no one does). We can also be happy. We can wear branded clothes and shoes, go on nice holidays, eat expensive meals, and most importantly, post it on social media for everyone to see. So you see, you can lose the battle, but you cannot afford to lose the war, and make no mistake, this is a full-fledged war!

Of course, there are no free lunches in this world. These belongings, meals, trips, and experiences cost money. The problem is, money is not evenly distributed in the world. We all have different means. In fact, at no other time in history, has there been such a stark divide between rich and poor. Lucky for us, this great invention called the credit card can 'solve' a lot of our problems. It doesn't really matter how much we can afford if we can make it look like we can. Hence, the reason why way too many people in this world are practically addicted to debt, running massive credit card balances, mostly accumulated by expenditures made solely to feed His Majesty, King Ego. And therein lies the moot point - none of those three things – marketing, social media, or credit are intrinsically bad. They have many practical uses too. The real problem is how we use them to manifest our internal insecurities, palpable deficiencies, and fragile egos.

But why is it so important for us to keep up with the Joneses? Like most things in life, there isn't a simple answer, but here are some popular views, including mine. Much of it is attributable to our historical roots, where being better was very often a matter of life and death. The slowest guy wouldn't eat or would get eaten, so the faster one was, the better. A bigger and stronger guy would be considered a better partner than a skinny one because he could provide better protection. The stronger warrior would survive, while the weaker could be offered as tribute to the gods if he lost the fight. Like I mentioned earlier, natural selection itself would weed out the inferior specimen. In this respect, we are not much different from animals. While peacocks fan out their feathers and lions flaunt their manes to attract mates, which ultimately is required for the species' survival, human beings use material possessions to demonstrate status and superiority.

Looking beyond our primal instincts, one of the foundational theories in social psychology is Leon Festinger's social comparison theory[54]. Over 70 years ago, Festinger concluded that we tended to evaluate our status and abilities compared to others to define ourselves. A key message of his theory is that we use others as a yardstick since there is rarely an objective criterion to measure ourselves against. We cannot define ourselves in isolation, so we need to look at ourselves in relation to others to answer the question, "Who am I?". This makes a lot of sense, right? How would we know if we are smart or not, wealthy or not, funny or not? If I sit an exam and score 100/120, am I smart? I guess I would be if the average score on the exam was 80/120, but maybe not so smart if the average was 110/120. If I were a football striker and scored 20 goals in the season, would that make me a great striker or a terrible one? If most strikers scored only 10 on average, I would be the former, but if they scored 40, I would be well below average. If I earned £80 000 a year, should I consider myself well off or not? Again, the answer to this question is based on what the average person in my social circle, company, or line of work earns, depending on who my benchmark is. An interesting study was performed in Sweden a few years ago. As part of it, people were given a hypothetical choice between:

1. Earning less in absolute terms, but still more than others
2. Earning more in absolute terms, but less than others

What do you think most of the people preferred? What would you prefer? The results showed that the overwhelming majority of people opted for the former option[55]. This is because we value ourselves concerning others. Earning more than others gives us a sense of achievement, while the opposite scenario reduces our perception of self-worth.

A little healthy competition or comparison to find out where we stand compared to others is not necessarily a bad thing. I would even argue that it is beneficial. The problem emerges when we are adamant about competing with the Joneses, or the Kardashians these days, to feed our egos. We then engage in a mindless and precarious race to the bottom, where all we do is driven by an irrational desire to win this imaginary competition. Our animalistic predilections take control of our decisions, which is why we buy that even larger TV, book an even further holiday, maybe even try and sabotage a colleague's promotion over us. We may not show or act on our vile impulses, but losing this competition makes a dent in our egos as it raises some uncomfortable questions in our heads.

- Steve and I started work at the same time and at the same level. Steve got promoted, but I didn't. Is Steve better than me?
- Sarah and I grew up together. Now, Sarah is Head of Marketing in a large multinational company, wears branded clothes, and goes on exotic cruises every year, whereas I barely make ends meet. Where did I go wrong?
- Stuart is a few years younger than me but already has a good career, a nice car, a loving wife, and two kids, while I am almost 40, single, and stuck at my miserable job. Am I a total failure?

Ouch, that hurts, doesn't it? Social comparison is great when we come out on top, but can deflate us when we are at the receiving end of things. This is why comparison is a double-edged sword. It is this thing, which makes us happy about others' successes, but also a little upset with ourselves. It is this little nagging feeling, which on one side thinks "great for them", while on the other cannot help but ask, "why isn't this me?". It certainly isn't the most flattering side of our personalities, but it is a part of who we are. Does this make us bad people? Not necessarily. We are used to thinking in binaries, but there is a lot more to us than this. We are the single most complex creature known to us and are an intertwined combination of good and bad, successes and failures. We cannot stop comparing to others or being a little jealous from time to time, and maybe we shouldn't; we just need to learn to live with it.

22

Chapter 16 – Selling Happiness

"Suicide is kinda dumb to me. If I wanna kill myself I will. It's not hard to die, I could do it like right now. But why is everybody pretending like everything's ok, Everything's not ok. We are more connected than we've ever been, But I feel more alone than I've ever been. "

- Donald Glover

If someone came to you and asked you if it were fine for them to feel down, sad, and disappointed, what would you tell them? I assume the answer would be "yes, of course". What if they then asked you whether you were a hypocrite? What would you answer then? Again, I would assume that the answer to this question would be "no" because not many people consider themselves hypocrites or think too much about it. I would argue that anyone who answered these two questions as per my assumption is indeed hypocritical. I count myself as part of this group. This is because we tend to be oblivious to the fact that it is perfectly normal sometimes to fail, make mistakes, or simply feel down. But we are living in an era when we are simply addicted to the idea of happiness. This would be a good time to clarify an important clarification – we are not addicted to happiness itself, but to its idea or perception.

Looking at the developed and large parts of the developing world, where the majority of the population live in a decent environment (I would qualify this simply as not deprived of basic necessities), most people these days attribute a lot greater role to happiness in their lives. I guess this is a sign of those parts of the world having reached a point of their development where they do not have to toil hard to make ends meet. I remember the lectures on Maslow's hierarchy of needs from my management studies at university[56]. For those who are unversed with this theory, it refers to a hierarchy of the needs of the society, usually graphically represented as a pyramid where the most primal needs like food, water, shelter, and safety are at the bottom. On the other hand, the feelings of harnessing our latent potential and achieving personal goals are at the top of this pyramid. As we meet our needs at a lower level, we climb our way to the next one. These days, we seem to be more focused on our happiness, which is a fairly accurate indicator that we are comfortable with our lives (comfortable, not satisfied). Happiness is often stated as one of the top things people wish for in their lives. It does not defy common sense because happiness is all-encompassing. We could wish for more money, but there is no guarantee this will make us happier; we could ask for a better job, but it might not necessarily give us the satisfaction we are looking for; we could ask for health, which is very important, but being healthy alone is no guarantee we will be content with our lives. Happiness, meanwhile, seems to cover all bases.

However, the big question is if we are all so focused on happiness and we are constantly in its pursuit, are we indeed happy? It is not an easy question to answer as levels of happiness cannot be measured in isolation. Hence, researchers often use a reference point in the past to ask this question slightly differently – are we happier today than we were 50, 100, or 500 years ago? Needless to say, this is a fairly contentious topic, and the results are generally quite inconclusive due to methodological differences. However, many studies have revealed worrying tendencies in depression and loneliness, especially among younger people. A lot of this is due to the social comparison we covered in the previous chapter. Far-reaching social platforms have exacerbated this menace beyond measure,[58,59] as they make it virtually impossible to compete against the whole world – the beautiful Instagram models (despite the huge discrepancies between pictures and real-life appearance in many cases), the successful entrepreneurs, the pumped-up fitness models.

I focus on children or teenagers as these impressionable individuals are extremely susceptible to social comparisons. We tend to grow out of it a little when growing older, but not completely. We just shift the goal post and start comparing on different criteria. Was colleague X promoted ahead of us at work, did neighbour Y buy a better car, and did that random person Z on our social network buy a bigger house than ours? Not much of a muchness, is it? Maybe, we just learn how to mask it a bit better. Put the veneer of a fake smile and pretend, even when we know that our blood is boiling and we can't do a damn thing about it.

Before I am being accused of being a perennial pessimist/cynic, let me clarify. There is nothing wrong with celebrating successes or demonstrating happiness. In fact – we must do. What is problematic is that we tend to share our highs and not our lows - who has got promoted at work, who has attained a qualification, who has won some award, whose son or daughter has graduated from university, who has gone on the best holiday, who has bought a car or a house, etc. All of these comparisons create a very distorted view of life. We all know our wins and our problems, but all we see from the outside world is the good, without the bad and the ugly. And it is this chasm between what we perceive in others, versus what we know about ourselves, gives us the impression that our lives are inferior, that we aren't good enough and constantly playing catch up. Consequently, it impacts our happiness and how we feel. The concept is pretty much the same as the iceberg illustration, where we only see the success above the water (the tip of the iceberg), but not the struggles underneath. So, what can we do? Consider exploring these options:

Stop Comparing

Many life coaches (which seem so popular as a profession these days) or other happiness experts would argue that we should stop measuring our worth concerning others and focus on ourselves. No doubt, this is good advice. But hear out my contention. This is like saying – you just need to keep practising and start running faster and faster, and you will beat Usain Bolt in a race. At most times, we already know when it should be done to achieve something. The problem is following through. As discussed in the previous chapter, we frequently compare ourselves to others due to evolutionary and psychological reasons. Changing our nature lies on the continuum between hard and impossible. Yes, some people have mastered this "art" of achieving true happiness by focusing on themselves alone, but I am not talking about the chosen few who have lady luck on their side. Every rule has an exception, but these few lucky people are exactly that – an exception, not the rule.

Retaliate

This is what most of us do because it is easy, and let's be honest here, we love the easy way out. Social comparison is a race in which everyone is trying their best to finish first. Every little win – promotion, success, happy moment, exemplifies superiority. And here is the paradox. What makes us happier is not the win itself. It is all those "Congratulations!", all the likes, and the shares, and the comments, the fact that all those people found out, and a little sense of triumphalism. We measure our worth by ingratiating ourselves to our loved ones and are at the mercy of others' positive reactions to such an extent that we even lose sight of what truly matters. I allude to it as our fixation with external validation. The outcome of that is – the perception of the happiness we create in others becomes more important than happiness itself. Once we establish that, the rest is easy – the race is on! Invite some friends over to showcase the new leader sofa or re-done patio, drop a few casual comments during the chit chat with a colleague by the coffee machine, update a few statuses on social media, etc. Then, of course, if we do it, so does everyone else, and before long, we have a perfect vanity storm – a world where we are all in the game of faking success and happiness. This is a dangerous game to play because winners are few and far between. We end up deluding ourselves, losing track of what matters to us, and spend a lot of time, money, and effort in the process, not to mention the concomitant psychological dent it inflicts.

Accept That We Cannot Always Be Happy

There is another, not so simple, but efficient solution – we just accept that this is all fake and we are just not meant to be constantly happy and content. There are two sides to this, which, in my view, reinforce each other. First, acknowledge that this is all a game of fakeness. There is nothing real in social media or what people do about it. We do it to flatter our ego, simple as that. Jim bought an expensive car but has been sitting at home, feeling miserable for the last three months because all his social life budget now goes into paying the car lease instalments. Alice worked her socks off to get that coveted promotion but did not even realise when her husband started cheating on her with Katie next door. Steve posted a hundred brilliant pictures from the Caribbean to show he was a high-flyer. But as he couldn't afford it, he shared a room with four other strangers and began packing up food for home to save some money. Every tip of the iceberg has a lot below the surface that people do not show. Once we see past the façade, the illusion of greatness others try to sell to us, starts crumbling down, and the disparity between their and our not-so-perfect lives starts shrinking.

The second part of this solution is simply accepting that we are not meant to be constantly happy. Like I mentioned earlier in the chapter, we are growing addicted to happiness. Being happy is great, it is probably the best thing that can ever happen to us, but a permanent state of happiness is like a maliciously deceptive illusion we would do well to avoid. We are probably only happy and feel fulfilled 10% of the time. Similarly, we might be upset or unhappy about something like 10% of the time, but for the vast majority of the time (you guessed it - 80%), we are just in a stable, medium state of mind. I am making these numbers up, by the way, but it feels about right. I do not expect everyone to agree with me, but I don't think we are meant to be constantly happy. Many people preach doing what makes you happy and pursuing happiness in everything you do, but if you are completely honest to yourself, you would agree that it is just not realistic. Are we chasing a

Chimera? Personally speaking, I have accepted that life is not meant to be about perpetual happiness, and I should treasure it when it comes. The rest of the time, I have to get up early, work, do chores, none of which, I have to admit, gives me particular pleasure (even though I like my job), but I have to do it if I want to eat and have a normal life. Even if you do not completely agree with me, it helps manage expectations about happiness and the lower our expectations, the happier we can be – this is one of my fundamental truths of life.

Note: Happiness is a complex thing, and it is influenced by many factors including, but not limited to our social status, amount of sleep, income, the time we spend doing what we like, social interactions, etc. In this chapter, I have decided to only cover the social comparison aspect attributed to the postulations of social psychology.

23

Chapter 17 - Fear of Change and the Status Quo

"The riskiest thing we can do is just maintain the status quo."
- Robert Iger

On 9th March 1934, a boy was born in a family of farmers in a small village 200 km west of Moscow. Life back then wasn't easy, especially when the Germans occupied his village during World War II. He was only seven years old back then. They burned down his school, pausing his education, and took his family home. After a German soldier tried hanging his younger brother on a tree using the kid's own scarf, the boy decided to become a saboteur and help the Red Army.

Towards the end of the war, when the German soldiers were retreating, he assisted in finding mines buried in the roads. It would not be farfetched to infer that this was not the kind of childhood most of us know today. In 1946, he returned to school, showing interest in Maths, sciences, and aviation. A few years later, at the age of 21, the boy volunteered at a local flying club as an air cadet.

Fast-forward a few years. The day was 11th April 1961, in the midst of the Cold war, with the USA and USSSR competing for supremacy across virtually anything. In the evening, the now grown-up boy played pool with a friend, while happily discussing their lives. He went to bed early that night, waking up at 5:30 the next morning[60]. Less than four hours later, he would make history by becoming the first man to go into outer space. His name was Yuri Gagarin.

Was it smooth sailing for him? Not by a long shot. The night before the flight, while doing some final weigh-ins, the support crew found out that the combined weight of Gagarin, his spacesuit and chair, was 13kg more than the permissible limit. They spent the night making last-minute modifications to reduce the weight. A few minutes before the flight itself, the capsule's door, holding Gagarin himself, wouldn't shut, requiring further changes. At 09:07, the engines roared to life, but that wasn't everything. Gagarin's descend module could not fully separate from the instrument module on the way back to Earth. This made his capsule spin out of control. It took a few minutes for the two parts to fully detach, during which the temperature was rising, threatening to incinerate the pod and Gagarin himself. Finally, at 7 km above the ground, Gagarin managed to eject and parachuted to safety. The spacecraft was controlled from the ground throughout the flight because the crew was unsure about the impact of lack of gravity on the human body and Gagarin's ability to control the machine.

What Gagarin did was an extraordinary feat by any stretch of the imagination, the kind few people in the world or across history have had the opportunity to undertake. But it doesn't take going to space to fulfil our more mundane goals. Most people have some goals in life, some smaller, others larger. Goals are funny, just like the hedonic treadmill, which makes upward adjustments in our expectations and has us asking for more. We all know that our goals in life change regularly. You hit one, and another one immediately takes its place. This is how we are built, to always ask for more. If we were all happy with what we had, the world would have been a very different place, and we would probably still be living in caves. But, going from point A, where we are now, to point B, where we want to be, requires a change, a transformation of sorts. It takes doing something more, something different, going out of our comfort zone, and pushing boundaries. Change, by definition, involves an element of risk. Reluctance to change or take this risk is often the main impediment that prevents people from taking a leap of faith and reaching for the skies. As the famous ice hockey player Wayne Gretzky famously said, "You miss 100% of the shots you don't take". Most people would probably agree with this statement, but continue to be resistant to change. We all know someone (or maybe we are that someone) who hates their life or certain aspects of their life. They have been married for twenty or thirty years and cannot stand their partner anymore but would not leave them because they are ambivalent about their choices and future outcomes. Will they be alone for the rest of their lives? Or let's say they have been stuck in the same role at work for a few years, causing them to feel perennially dissatisfied. Is it worth changing the role because they at least know what they are doing at this stage? There are various reasons for our desire to remain in our comfort zone – status quo bias, fear of the unknown, risk-aversion, etc. Let's look into some of these.

The Status Quo Bias

We all have a comfort zone. It is different for everyone, but it is that beaten track, which provides some level of control and comfort. We love our comfort zones for a few reasons:

1. Familiarity – we follow an established routine, we do this, and then we do that. Most of the time, we do things in autopilot mode without putting any thought behind it.
2. Ease – by extension, knowing our environment and routine, makes things easy. It takes lesser mental energy to follow what you know, than making new conscious decisions or staying alert in an unknown environment.
3. Sense of control – the more we know something, the more we feel we can control it. Truth be told, we love

being in control…or at least being under the impression we are. Introducing a change entails relinquishing control over the situation. Never an easy process!

The status quo has us in a gentle grip that provides comfort and a sense of security. It is like the Lotus tree in Greek mythology, whose fruits caused laziness, forgetfulness, and apathy. It would capture Odysseus and his men under his sweet aromatic spell and entrap them on an island, where they would feel content and distracted from their mission, never wanting to leave.

Against this backdrop, there is no surprise that we are often reluctant to come out of our comfort zone. In social psychology, this is known as a status quo bias. If our ambition and motivation to achieve something more are the engines that push us to move forward and explore new horizons, the status quo bias is the anchor, which holds us back, keeping us in calm waters.

Fear of the unknown

This is the "what if" question. "I hate my job, but what if the next one is even worse"? "I want to take up this new side project, but what if it fails"? "I want to invest my savings somewhere, as those interest rates are really not doing me any favour, but what if I lose everything"? There probably isn't anything more natural to us than being afraid of the unknown. Many animals prefer sticking to their usual habitat and only venture out if their very survival is threatened e.g., food or water in the area has evaporated, and they need to go further to find some. Yes, we are not zebras or antelopes, but our survival instinct works similarly.

It is often reported that children of alcoholics marry alcoholics later in life. On the surface, this is very counterintuitive. Those children are exposed to neglect (if they are lucky) and often to verbal and physical abuse. Later on in life, many of them exhibit the propensity to judge themselves harshly, inability to relax, tendency to isolate, difficulty forming relationships, etc. So, logic dictates that they would know better than marrying an alcoholic later in life. The reality, however, is somewhat different. Experience suggests that they are attracted to alcoholics as they take comfort in familiarity. They have seen drunk behaviour often enough to know what to expect and, like in some twisted horror movie, it just feels normal to stay. Matthew Salis, a writer, speaker, and former alcoholic from Denver, described his relationship with his wife (a daughter of an alcoholic) as follows: "My wife married me because my alcoholic behaviour didn't sufficiently repulse her. She'd seen it before, so it didn't shock or threaten her. My behaviour as an active drinker might not have been acceptable, but it was familiar to my bride. And familiarity breeds comfort"[61]. His story perfectly fits the old adage that the devil we know is better than the devil we don't.

We also tend to fear the unknown due to biological reasons. A study from a group of researchers, published in 2016, demonstrated that the unknown is more stressful than knowing something is going to have negative consequences[62]. For example, not knowing if you have passed an exam is more stressful for people than knowing they have failed. The same applies to interviewing for a job, being made redundant, running late for a flight, not knowing if you will catch it or not, etc. Once you get the bad news, we get to terms with them, and after a period of disappointment, we get over them, but the uncertainty really stresses us out by spiking the release of dopamine in the striatum.

Loss Aversion

Coined by two leading scholars in behavioural economics and decision-making, Amos Tversky and Daniel Kahneman, loss aversion relates to human preference to avoid losses compared to equivalent gains[63]. Put simply, it means we would hate losing £100 a lot more than winning £100. This has been proven by brain scans of subjects experiencing equivalent gains and losses. The striatum shows activity in both cases, but this is more pronounced when presented with a loss scenario.

Have you ever wondered what the purpose of those free trial periods for various subscription-based services is? The likes of a 7-day free trial, first-month free trial, etc. Quite nice of companies to be offering a free service, don't you think? I have no qualms in pointing out that I don't believe they do it out of the goodness of their hearts. While it provides the chance to check out the service and see if you like it, there is a significant psychological element. Once we have the service through the free subscription, we would hate to see it go (loss aversion, remember?).

Loss aversion has significant implications for understanding our reluctance to move away from our comfort zone. When we face the possibility of a loss on one side and a potential gain on the other side, theory suggests that we are more likely to stay where we are and avoid the potential loss, unless the benefits are disproportionately larger. In light of the status quo preservation, this means that to make a leap of faith, the potential gains need to decisively overweigh the possibility of losing what we have now. This suggests an innate preference to keep things stable and avoid losses.

Of course, there are marked differences in the extent of people's loss aversion due to socio-economic and cultural factors. For example, studies show wealthier people and those in power are more likely to take risks and overcome the loss aversion bias[64]. This is due to the handy use of their wealth and connections, which can help them bounce back if things go south. Similarly, a large-scale study, undertaken across 53 countries globally, shows drastic differences in loss aversion between collectivist (e.g. African societies) and individualist (e.g. Eastern European societies). The theory posits that loss aversion in collectivist societies is lower due to reliance on social groups to help out if things don't exactly work out as expected[65].

Sunk Cost Fallacy

In business and accounting, a sunk cost refers to a cost that has been incurred and can no longer be recovered. For example, you want to look into the possibility of taking a mortgage and buying a property, something that way too many people are painfully familiar with. Like most people, you might not be a real estate or a mortgage advisor, so you decide to book an appointment with a mortgage advisor for a specific consultation fee of, let's say £200. After the consultation has taken place and you have a better idea of what you could afford and how much you will have to pay each month, you decide to either go ahead and buy a property or not. Regardless of your future decision, the £200 is gone; you have spent the money and cannot have it back, so your £200 is now a sunk cost for all practical purposes.

Good business and project management sense suggests that we should not factor in sunk costs in our future decisions, that we should drop a project when costs outweigh the potential benefits, and that we should also drop a project when there is no longer a solid business justification for it. The logic is simple – we are where we are, we have spent X amount of money, time, energy, and other resources, which are no longer recoverable. Thus, we should just stop there and avoid incurring even more costs in delivering something we don't need or no longer offers any material benefit. As far as logical reasoning goes, that makes sense. However, as mentioned quite a few times before in this book, we are not that rational or smart. Once we start investing in something, be it money, time, energy, hopes, or whatever, we need to get something in return.

Dropping a project halfway through serves as a big reality check that we have failed, and we have nothing to show for it, but going home with our tail between our legs. Not very good for our self-esteem, is it? Let's try and understand this better with an example. You are planning a nice holiday with your partner and book through a travel agency, which lets you pay a non-refundable deposit of £300 on booking, with the balance not due until closer to the time. You happily pay the deposit, but you and the partner get separated a couple of months before the actual travel. The travel agency comes to you and asks for the balance of £1200, but you have no one to go with. You ask your friends, but they all have other plans for this time or are not keen on the destination. At this point, you should probably take the hit, write off the deposit, and leave it there. But you remind yourself of the fact that you have already paid £300 and can't just let it go, can you? Lucky for you, your mum is happy to go. She will happily cover her part of the trip and the small fee to change the name on the ticket. Certainly, not the holiday you envisioned, but oh well, at least you didn't lose the deposit.

If it makes you feel better, don't worry about it, we all do it, and if history is anything to go by, even very well paid and smart government officials do it too. Take the creation of Concorde, for example. This was a joint initiative between the British and French governments to launch a supersonic plane flying across the Atlantic for under an hour. In 1962, the two governments agreed to fund the project at an expected cost of around £150-170 million and delivery by 1970. By 1973, the development costs (already spent) were estimated at around £1.065 billion, in addition to the fact that they were already years behind the go-live date. By this point, both governments had realised the project was a huge commercial disaster but since they had already invested too much to stop there, and were embarrassed after sending over £1 billion of taxpayer money in vain, going ahead with the plan was the only feasible option. The planes eventually went into service in 1976, at which point the programme's total costs were estimated at around £1.3 billion[66]. Eventually, it turned out to be a commercial disaster, and Concorde was eventually retired.

You probably wonder what this was to do with the status quo and our reluctance to change it. Here is what you may want to know. Like the British and French governments in the Concorde project, we invest time, money, and energy into what we do. The longer we do it, the more invested we become. As a snowballing effect, the harder it gets to drop it and start doing something new. There probably isn't a simple person who hasn't thought they wanted to change their job but hesitated due to their reluctance to abandon everything they have worked for on the current job behind. We are unhappy with what we do and want a change, but keep going back to the many years we have already invested in the organisation. We are so close to the desired promotion, which will make all the difference, that we begin to question the merits of a job change. Sadly, this cycle almost always repeats year after year. The same applies to every other aspect of our lives, which we could possibly change, but we are too invested in them already. Oh, if only things were simpler...

Risk-Aversion

Risk is inherent to every change. If abandoning the status quo requires a change, this would carry a certain amount of risk by extension. By nature, most people are risk-averse, i.e., we prefer certain outcomes to risky outcomes and low-risk outcomes to high-risk outcomes. We usually talk about risk aversion in a financial context and how much financial risk one is comfortable carrying, but the risk does not have to be financial. It relates to the possibility of losing time, efforts, relationships, hopes, and integrity, among other things. A study shows that six in ten Britons (i.e. 60%) admit they are afraid of taking risks[67]. This is not surprising and not only applicable to Britons, although there are marked cultural differences. Our brains are wired to prefer the status quo and the comfort of what we know, to taking risks. They are built to keep us safe instead of taking risks in the pursuit of a better life.

Needless to say, risk can also be expressed as a continuum with different people having different risk appetites or the ability to carry risk along this continuum. What could be considered a very reasonable risk to take by one, could be completely out of the question for another. Why would one run the possibility of losing something, if there is no opportunity for a gain? Usually, the higher the risk, the higher the potential gain.

Risk-aversion is status quo's best friend. Status quo loves the way things are – stable, easy, risk-free. This is where risk-aversion thrives best. So, if we are naturally predisposed to risk aversion, change does not come easily. An additional factor in play here is also our tendency to often exaggerate both the probability and impact of things going wrong. Based on the probability of occurrence, large cataclysmic events, rare as they might be, leave a deep scar in our minds and impact our future decisions a lot more than they should.

Put simply, this is where we always think the worst would happen. One such event was the terrorist attacks on 9/11 (or as our fellow Americans would express it 11/9). A truly tragic event in the US history, but one that is unlikely to be a regular occurrence and happen again shortly after. Yet, the perception that planes are easy to hijack and make air travel look a lot less safe than it is, caused many Americans to cut down flying and drive instead. Ironically, passenger air miles decreased by roughly 16% in the three months after the attack, while driving and the number of road fatalities increased. The German professor Gerd Gigerenzer, estimated the number of fatalities, caused by more people driving over the next twelve months after the attack at 1 595[68]. This was due to people overestimating the possibility of a similar terrorist event in the near future and retreating to what is perceived as a safer way to travel. In everyday life, his safer option is the status quo.

Factors Impacting Our Status Quo Preference

Above are just some of the reasons why we tend to feel more comfortable with what we have now and be reluctant to change it even if we are not always happy. I use the word comfortable here to keep things as they are, not necessarily implying that we don't want to change the situation. However, many different factors influence our attitudes towards the status quo and risk. I will not go into detail here, but some of the common ones are: upbringing, culture, observed behaviour from others, genetic, socio-economic factors, etc. We already touched on the cultural and socio-economic factors briefly earlier in the chapter. Attitude towards risk is also acquired from our parents and others in our social circle (see the chapter on attitude formation for more details). Motivation is another big one worth mentioning. Yes, we are risk and loss-averse, which, if we refer back to Tversky and Kahneman's theory, means we would not risk what we have today for an equally large potential gain. However, we are a lot more likely to do it if the gain is large enough (i.e. providing larger motivation to engage in risk-taking behaviour). Additionally, Camelia Kuhnen, a neuroeconomics and behavioural finance expert, had discovered a gene called DRD4, which regulates our hormone levels in the reward centre of our brains, determining how risk-averse or not one is. Her findings suggest that the prevalence of this hormone in some investors makes them up to 25% more risk-prone than others[69].

Influences are so any and diverse that it is virtually impossible to find two people with the exact same risk attitude. This explains why we still sometimes engage in risk-taking behaviour and why some people are more likely to stay in their comfort zone than others despite our inborn preference for safety and status quo preservation.

How to Get Better?

Only because we have a natural inclination for something does not mean we cannot change it. The general consensus is that change is good. We just need to break the status quo and allow ourselves to dream. Doing so can have a hugely beneficial impact on our lives. I am not advocating jumping off a cliff in the hope that you could fly. A well calculated risk required to make a change is good, but too much of it could have the exact opposite effect.

1. **Frame the options differently**. We already discussed how our brains hate losing. We hate losing a lot more than we love gaining. We can use this to our advantage by tricking our brains into thinking of the status quo as a loss. Here is a remarkably simple example. You hate your job, which is currently paying £50 000 a year. You have been doing it for a few years. You know it inside out and have off-the-shelf solutions to pretty much any problem. Career progression isn't great, but things can get streamlined. A friend tells you about another role where they work, which pays £55 000 and you would be a good fit. Like every other job, though, you have to go through the painful process of recruitment, screening, the whole admin shebang, and then a few months

of training and getting up to speed until you are comfortable again. You start weighing pros and cons, and for the sake of argument, let's say your key motivation for the new job is money, but the cons are barriers to change, the need to acclimatise to a new environment, and the possibility of the job being worse than the existing one. At least yours is stable. Some quick Math tells you that, £5 000 a year extra is just now worth it. Factor in the additional tax, break it down to what this means in terms of monthly salary, and the incremental gain is roughly £250 a month; not bad, but not a life changer either. With this, you could probably afford a couple more family dinners out a month, and a few more drinks out with friends. The status quo bias would tell many in this situation to stay where they are and keep things simple. In this case, the riskier option (the new job) is presented as a potential gain against keeping things as they are (the current option). Here is the key thing: flip this around to present the current option as a loss compared to the alternative (the new job). What if staying where you are would be a loss of £250 every month compared to the alternative? And, this loss would only be accumulating every month. You could end up losing quite a lot. This little trick alone can increase the motivation to change the status quo.

2. **Do a reality check from time to time**. It is very easy to get sucked up into a habit and keep things as they are, just because they have been this way for a long time. But

just because this is how it has been so far, does not necessarily mean, this is how it must be. Challenge the status quo. Ask yourself: "Am I getting what I want and need from the current situation, or is there a potential to make things better"? If there is no justification to keep doing what you do, drop it and start something new; don't be like Concorde.

3. **Plan and assess risks.** We fear the unknown because it is *unknown*. Shedding light into the darkness is the best way to see what lies beyond our current sight. Assess the risks and consider how they can be mitigated. At the surficial level, the idea of risks quickly sways us towards inaction, but few risks in this world are uncontrollable. Risk avoidance (i.e. not taking the risk in the first place) is just one of the ways to manage risks successfully. There are plenty of other strategies we can employ to reduce the possibility of a risk occurring. Reduce the impact once it does occur, or transfer the risk onto someone else (e.g. taking out insurance).

4. **Let go of the idea what everything must be controlled**. For many people, the idea that doing something else or different means relinquishing some control over the situation, which can be a scary thought bad enough to kindle bouts of hysteria. The perception that we have more control over something because we know it better is what makes us clutch onto the status quo and forego so many potential opportunities. Complete control is an illusion. The world is an unpre-

dictable place. We try to make sense of the chaos and improve our control over it, but it can never be tamed. Only when we embrace the part of it, outside of our control, can we reach for the skies.

5. **Keep sight of your goals**. Motivation is a powerful driver. It is easy to lose sight of what we are fighting when we cannot see the wood for the trees. Take a step back, remember your objectives, and determine if the current situation helps achieve them. If not, change.

6. **Baby Steps**. We must recognise that we are predisposed towards keeping the status quo. It is not easy to overcome our loss and risk aversion, but we do not have to do it overnight. Push your limits one step at a time.

In conclusion, I am a strong believer in taking risks and pushing boundaries on the way to success. The world has evolved to this point and keeps evolving, because of people who have dared to dream and see beyond what is here and now. However, as we have seen, there are many psychological and evolutionary factors that work in tandem to maintain the status quo, which, to my mind, is one of our most formidable adversaries. There is a very simple reason for this – to improve our likelihood of survival. However, these factors are decreasingly relevant to the modern world, as we are not in a constant battle for survival, and progress is only possible when we push hard enough to counteract our instincts.

That being said, the first step in the right direction is to recognise the existence of our fears and predisposition towards the status quo. And even after this, it doesn't necessarily get easier. The purpose of this chapter is to shed light on this topic, which is such a big part of our lives. We don't always think of our lives in this way, but every day wherein nothing changes is a day when we have once again chosen the status quo. This is not necessarily a bad thing, of course. Stability is indeed a requirement for survival, and if we apply the Pareto rule 80% of the time, we will choose the status quo, but it is the remaining 20% when we don't that will make all the difference. I will conclude with a nice quote from the American theologian William Shedd, "A ship is safe in harbour, but that is not what ships are for".

24

Chapter 18 – Greed

Here, more than elsewhere, I saw multitudes
to every side of me; their howls were loud
while, wheeling weights, they used their chests to push.
They struck against each other; at that point,
each turned around and, wheeling back those weights,
cried out, 'Why do you hoard?" "Why do you squander?
- Divine Comedy: Inferno – Dante Alighieri

Let's start by looking into three short stories.

1. Kenneth Lay was by all counts and public opinion one of the most successful people in the US. Having been appointed as CEO of Enron in 1985, it took him only ten years to turn the company into one of the world's

largest, most successful, and respectable companies. Under his management, and with the help of Jeffrey Skilling (who took charge as the CEO in 2001) and Andrew Fastow (company CFO), Kenneth Lay managed to turn Enron into the God of Wallstreet. At its peak, the company had a market capitalization of $60 billion and reported a turnover of $138 billion for the first nine months of 2001[70]. For comparison purposes, around $60 billion is the estimated GDP of Belarus for 2020, according to the World Bank[71]. There are many corporates with market capitalization higher than most countries' GDP worldwide, especially with behemoths like Apple, Amazon, and Microsoft, but this still gives a pretty good picture of Enron's size at the time (this was 20 years ago). The company was voted America's Most Innovative Company by Fortune magazine for six consecutive years between 1996 and 2001. The trio at the helm of the company was indeed extremely creative and innovative... in how they hid corporate debt, manipulated earning and share prices, and altered its financials. Innovative they were, but for all the wrong reasons. On 2nd Dec 2021, Enron filed for bankruptcy, becoming the largest corporate bankruptcy in the history of America to that point. Investors lost billions, and thousands of employees lost their job, some of them even their lives. Yet, Enron paid its top executives $681 million in the same year, with Kenneth Lay alone grabbing $67.4 million[72].

2. Norberto Odebrecht was a Brazilian engineer, businessman, and philanthropist of German descent. Born in 1920, he founded a construction company - Norberto Odebrecht Construtora Ltda at the age of 24. He and his descendants, who later took on the company's management, must have been a bunch of outstandingly savvy businessmen. The company ended up becoming the largest engineering and contracting company in Latin America because under their leadership. By 2010, it had 181 000 employees worldwide. But similar to Enron, this growth was partly attributed to some questionable practices. In 2016, the company was involved in what was branded by the US Department of Justice as the "largest foreign bribery case in history". Between 2001 and 2016, the company paid nearly $800 million in bribes across Latin America to secure lucrative government contracts across the continent[73]. This involved one-third of Brazil's senators. The company CEO at the time admitted that some part of the donation made to candidates for presidents in the 2014 Brazil elections was illegal. In 2018, the president of Peru was forced to resign amid allegations related to the company. The vice president of Ecuador was sent to prison. These are just some of the hundreds of political figures who received generous care packages by the firm in return for political favours and lucrative contracts, at the expense of the wider public good.

3. It is another sunny day in the African savanna. A group of antelopes is herded under the trees, hiding from the scorching sun. A lioness spots the antelopes and prowls towards them, ever so stealthily, staying low to the ground and keeping its eyes fixated on its prey. Its muscles tense with every step, inching closer to the herd. Having gotten sufficiently close, the lioness launches itself forward, causing havoc among the surprised antelopes. As they run for their lives, a thick cloud of dust lifts above the ground. A single antelope seems to have strayed from the rest of the herd, making it an even easier prey, and letting natural selection take its normal course. The lioness pounces, sticking its mighty sharp claws into the antelope's body. By the time the dust settles, it is all over.

What do these three stories have in common? Kenneth Lay, the South American politicians, and the lioness wanted to safeguard their myopic interest. In that sense, humans are very similar to animals. There are, however, significant differences. Unlike humans, an animal cannot comprehend the wider implications of its actions. It acts on pure instinct. However, we are endowed with the capacity to project ourselves in the future, to act in our interest beyond here and now. We can picture ourselves laying on a yacht deck, sipping mojitos, while servants run around, attending to our every need, or having grand monuments commemorating our legacy for the generations to come. It is this capacity, which subverts self-interest into unabated avarice.

Like most things in life, self-interest is beneficial to humanity in moderation. It is a continuum along which we are all plotted, ranging from altruism and selflessness at one end to pure greed, selfishness, and megalomania at the other. In this chapter, like in all previous ones, I will adopt a human perspective, trying to understand this intrinsic inclination to serve our self-interest first and foremost, look at scenarios when this could be useful or not, and what this means for each one of us.

Greed is one of those topics that doesn't get discussed much in everyday life unless some mega scandal blows out and gets into the public spotlight. We don't openly talk about money, salaries, and our financial cravings (greed has many facets. For this chapter, I will focus on the most obvious ones – greed for money and power). Ask someone what they want, and they will likely tell you something like health, happiness, and friendship. One thing that is often on people's minds, but they would hardly ever say out loud, is MONEY! Why can't we admit it? We like money, and we like it a lot. We don't like money for the sake of it. We like it for what it can do for us – buy us a better car, sends us on a nice holiday, buy us some nice clothes, earn us status in society, and much more. One of the most important things money can buy us is freedom and independence, allowing us to take some time off work and just do something else, simply because we like it. For example, I want to go and do an MBA, but one of these easily costs

£30,000 or more at a top university in England, let alone sustenance costs, rent, bills, and other expenses one has while studying. The total bill is prohibitively high, so I must stick to my job. In one way or another, it always comes back to financial means. Even health, which, together with love, people traditionally argue that money cannot buy, can very much be bought today. Yes, we do not have a cure for every disease on Earth yet, but a lot more so today than we did in the past, and having access to top medical staff, advanced equipment, a lifesaving private operation abroad or experimental treatment often costs a lot of money.

Many of us crave good education, good healthcare, some freedom just to go away and do whatever we want for a while, and millions of material possessions. All these cost money, yet we hardly ever admit that money is what we want for some reason. I think a large contributing factor is the feeling of social shame. Greed has garnered a bad reputation in society. It is seen as vain, selfish, and void of higher purpose, so we wouldn't want to be associated with it. Some of this can be traced back to religious learning. In Christianity, avarice is one of the seven deadly sins. More specifically, it is seen as the idolatry of material and temporal possessions above the love for God and as a root cause of all evil. In *Divine Comedy*, Dante Alighieri, condemns greed as one the worst punishable sins, depicting sinners as spirits bound to roll enormous boulders across the fourth circle of hell for all eternity. Similarly, the Koran warns against the corruptive nature of wealth, and Buddhism sees cravings for material possessions as hurdles that stymie our enlightenment.

This said, even if we are not devout believers, it is easy to understand why greed is not seen particularly favourably in society, and we shy away from admitting we crave money. While I will look into some of the key arguments explaining why greed is natural and to some extent beneficial in the next section, I do not believe that it is necessarily a good thing in excess. I want to make a mere argument that it is pervasive in society, but often not recognised or admitted. This is because greed has two specific properties.

1. It is easily masked as ambition or determination, which are seen as positive qualities.
2. As a result of the previous point, it never applies to us! The bankers are greedy, the politicians are greedy, the corporate CEOs are greedy, but we are not, we are ambitious.

The Purpose of Greed

Greed has both biological and psychological foundations, making it a powerful force.

From a biological and evolutionary perspective, greed is codified in our DNA as a survival imperative. Without a certain amount of greed, individuals and communities were at the risk of running out of resources, thus reducing their survival chances. Unlike some animals, we are prone to hoard as a safety net against phases of scarce resources. Greed can also be seen from another evolutionary angle - our instincts not only apply to our survival today but also to perpetuating our genetic code throughout time[74]. This requires attracting more and better mates to give our offspring the best chances of survival. Because wealth is seen as an important sign of status and wellbeing, greed for more can be perceived as nothing more than a survival instinct.

In addition to this, there is also a psychological explanation. The pursuit of wealth, winning, and buying new possessions have been shown to stimulate the release of dopamine in the brain's reward system, which, in turn, makes us feel good. However, this "feel-good" factor is ephemeral, and we soon need another win or purchase to bring it back. It becomes addictive. Notably, various scientists have identified that greed activates similar pleasure pathways in our brains as addictions to drugs, food, or gambling[75]. This could explain a lot about successful people's never-ending cravings for more and more. There are numerous examples of wildly successful people, who never seemed to have gotten enough, ending up destroying their lives and everything they had built to date.

One such example is Rajat Gupta, who was the CEO of arguably the most reputable consulting company globally – McKinsey & Co. Undoubtedly an exceptionally yet flawed man. In the early 2000s, he served as a board member on various large organisations across the US, including Goldman Sachs, Proctor & Gamble, and American Airlines. His net worth was already estimated at above $100 million, but greed is a fickle b*tch. He was astutely rich enough to never worry about money throughout his lifetime and those of a few generations ahead. But that wasn't enough. Being surrounded by billionaires, Rajat wanted to get into the billionaires' circle. An opportunity presented itself in 2008 during the onset of the financial crisis. At the time, Goldman Sachs, one of the largest American investment banks, was struggling. That is when the legendary investor Warren Buffet decided to make a significant capital injection of $5 billion and resuscitate the dwindling share price. Often where the "Sage of Omaha" goes, others follow. Everyone with the faintest knowledge in finance knows that once Buffet invests in a company, others are bound to follow and share prices can only move in one direction - upwards. Initially, this was not in the public domain, but once Buffet broke the news to Goldman's board of directors, Rajat wanted to seize this opportunity. He immediately called his banker, placing a large buy order on Goldman's shares. When Buffet's investment was announced a few hours later, share price rose as expected and Rajat realised a hefty profit[76]. He didn't need this money, but he was not under the firm grip of greed, which can cripple even the smartest people's minds. It is an addiction.

When Can Greed be Good?

People don't often think about it, but a healthy dose of greed is good for the economy and the development of human civilization in its entirety. The argument goes that greed makes people always ask for more, always push for more to satisfy their hunger for wealth and prosperity. That pursuit of self-interest is what drives progress and ultimately benefits the whole society. This view has been perfectly summarised by the 18th century economist, widely regarded as the Father of Economics – Adam Smith. In his famous book *Wealth of Nations,* Smith famously concludes: "It is not from the benevolence of the butcher, the brewer, or the baker that we expect our dinner, but from their regard to their interest. We address ourselves, not to their humanity but to their self-love, and never talk to them of our necessities but their advantages.[77]" More recently, this notion of greed as an economic propeller was echoed by Gordon Gekko, a fictional character played by Michael Douglas in the 1987 movie *Wall Street,* who in his speech famously proclaims: "Greed, for lack of a better word, is good. Greed is right, greed works. Greed clarifies, cuts through, and captures the essence of the evolutionary spirit. Greed, in all its forms; greed for life, for money, for love, knowledge, has marked the upward surge of mankind.[78]" Of course, Wall Street was not a movie about upstanding citizens or caring about the greater good of society, but the quote does encapsulate the essence of the point I am trying to make.

The More Common, Ugly Side of Greed

Like everything else, greed must be confined to some boundaries to optimise its benefits. We can probably think of it in stages:

Stage 1 – healthy amount of greed, fully within legal and social boundaries, which promotes economic progress and general wellbeing. This is where most people are.

Stage 2 – not so healthy amount of greed, which is still within legal limits, but promotes obsession and alienation from those around us. This is where greed becomes an addition and becomes the ruler of most we do. This is sufficient to ruin people's personal lives and their relationships with others.

Stage 3 – the kind of greed, which makes people do stupid things and break all kinds of social norms and legal restrictions. The impact is often larger than one's own life and closest social circle.

It is that stage 3, which gets in the spotlight of public attention in high-profile cases. Corruption scandals, fraud, embezzlement, bankruptcies, all of these are prime examples of unrestrained greed. Unfortunately, such examples are countless around the world. Here are some facts and statistics:

- The World Bank estimates that businesses and individuals pay more than $1 trillion ($1 000 000 000 000) in bribes every year[79].
- According to a research study carried out by tax, advisory, and risk firm Crowe, together with the University of Portsmouth in 2019, fraud imposes a staggering cost burden of $5 trillion to the global economy every year[80].
- The United Nations Office on Drugs and Crime estimates the cost of money laundering in the world every year at between $800 billion and $2 trillion[81].
- Total fines paid by banks globally as a result of wrongdoing in 2020 alone was over $11 billion[82].

These are some of the scary statistics, which make the news all the time, the vast majority of which can be caused by human wrongdoing (as opposed to genuine mistakes). Not that I doubt people's good intentions, but I am inclined to believe that not much, if any of these, are attributable to modern-day Robin Hoods, who steal from the rich and give to the poor. Thus, I will stick to the cynical view: they are largely the result of good old greed.

Greed, The Bankers, and Everyone Else

Yet, one thing that often pains me is when people start talking about the greedy bankers and how they broke the world in 2008. This is probably because I work in finance myself and am under the endowment effect (valuing the industry more highly, because I associate with it). The bit that hurts me the most is the demonisation of financial professionals, while the holier-than-thou clan throwing stones at me is no better. It goes back to the good old hypocrisy, which is as rampant as ever. To be very clear – I am not saying that what happened in 2008 is right or that bankers acted ethically and responsibly; far from that. Instead, I contend that bankers are humans and are not immune to shortcomings like everyone else, probably just to a more pronounced degree, because they work more closely with money (often quite a lot of money). Many people outside the industry would have done the same thing had they been given the opportunity. Don't hate me yet, hear me out.

Acting in self-interest is human nature. Of course, not everyone would risk their job, their name, and their freedom in the pursuit of this self-interest, but many people would in given circumstances. It is easy for us to think that we would never do something stupid and put everything at risk no matter what happens. This is probably what many fraudsters think, too, before violating the law. There are so many factors at play, making it difficult for us to imagine a situation when we would myopically pursue our selfish interests at the expense of everything else. It is a complex interplay between various factors, how big the potential reward is, how likely is it we will get caught, what will happen if we do, what does our moral compass say, are we thinking straight in that particular moment or under emotions, are there social or other pressures, etc.

In his wonderful book *Predictably Irrational*[84], the professor in psychology and behavioural economics, Dan Ariely, describes performing a series of experiments, two of which I consider quite relevant to this topic. In one of them, he does a series of experiments on student's proclivity to cheat on a test for a monetary reward. The experiments were simple. He would give students tests and the ability to cheat but vary the degree to which students could get away with it and the financial reward. The results showed that when given a chance to cheat for a financial reward, many people did, and test results were higher than when there was no opportunity to cheat. So, people are likely to cheat if given the opportunity? Preposterous! In another experiment, he tested how people reacted when cold-headed versus when under emotions. For that specific experiment, the emotion was sexual arousal, but this is not the point. Again, probably unsurprisingly to many, many people said they wouldn't do something in a rational state of mind, but changed their minds when emotionally charged.

You do not have to be a psychology professor to reach the conclusions that Dan Ariely's experiments entertainingly demonstrated. Yet, it is always hard to imagine that we would do the same if we were given a similar opportunity to make quick money as those bankers. Keep in mind that while there were certainly high-profile fraud cases and acting irresponsibly leading up to the crisis, a lot of the money was made perfectly legally, exploiting the deregulated landscape. This is where things get even more interesting. If you wouldn't break a law to make some quick money, would you push boundaries, which could be morally questionable yet perfectly legal? Giving people with low-income mortgages, which they will likely not be able to service, is morally questionable, to say the least, but not illegal. Every mortgage earns you a commission, adding towards your own mortgage repayment, holiday, or whatever you want to spend your money on. You have your own family and expenditures to care about, after all. Would you do it?

Unfortunately, fraud, corruption, and greed are not prevalent only in finance, they are ubiquitous. Mining companies, which subsidise political campaigns and pay bribes to win extraction rights of countries' natural resources, building companies, which use cheap materials in infrastructure projects to bag a higher profit margin, politicians who accept bribes, accountants who massage balance sheets to inflate profits, car manufacturers which circumvent emission regulations, tech companies, with headquarters in offshore locations reducing tax bills... the list is endless and pervasive in every industry, not just banking.

Whenever any of the above happens, they immediately grab media attention and result in a public outcry against corrupt politicians, greedy bankers, and the whole capitalistic system, and rightly so. Any kind of fraud needs to be decried, punished accordingly, and measures are taken to curb the chances of it reoccurring. But unethical or illegal behaviour does not only happen on TV, what hits the media attention is just the high-profile cases. We look at a smug politician or a corporate CEO in an expensive suit and create a divide in our heads of us - the regular hardworking and honest people, and them - the rich and powerful who exploit the system. We often forget that they are people just like us. Often, they were part of us; not every rich or powerful person was born this way. The only difference is, when they f*** up, they f*** up big.

Consider the following data and examples. Have you heard of wardrobing? This is when you buy a good, use it and then return it. This is a fraudulent practice. Most commonly, it happens when people buy clothes, wear them with the tags, and return them to the store for a refund. A survey done in the UK shows that one in five (20%) wardrobes and the estimated total cost a year of this specific kind of fraud is £1.5 billion[85]. Similar data shows the cost of wardrobing in the US was $10.85 billion in 2014 alone[86]. Going back to Dan Ariely's test experiment, many of us would cheat in our self-interest and if given the opportunity. The cost of petty theft from retailers in the US and Europe alone is over $60 billion a year[87]. From this, we should deduct the cost of theft due to poverty and desperation in the context of greed. Some of these petty crimes could result from necessity (a starving person stealing bread, for example), but more often than not, they aren't. They are a result of greed and opportunism. Not unlike the people we see on TV, but on a lot smaller scale.

The Stealth Nature of Greed

I touched on this point briefly earlier in the chapter. Part of the reason we don't admit to being greedy is that we simply do not recognise it when it comes to us. Like with many other things, we have a blind spot for our shortcomings. The second point is, greed can easily be masked as positive qualities like ambition, determination, resilience, hunger to succeed. Part of the problem with recognizing it is that there isn't a precise definition of greed. One of the definitions is a strong desire to continuously get more of something. Quite generic, isn't it? Another source defines it as a selfish and excessive desire for more of something. Again, quite broad and also relative. How do you define excessive? It is all relative and comes down to perspective. Let me share the following example.

Cornelius Vanderbilt "The Commodore", was an American businessman in railroad building and shipping, and one of the richest men in American history. His biographer T. Stiles wrote about him, "He helped to create the corporate economy that would define the United States into the 21st century.[88]" There is a story about Mr. Vanderbilt finishing a series of business meetings, after which one of his advisors leans in, telling him that every deal he agreed had broken the law. Vanderbilt responded to this as follows: "...you don't suppose you can run a railroad under the statutes of the State of New York, do you? [89]"

They often say that the victors write history. Cornelius Vanderbilt went down the history as one of the most successful and richest men. His defiance against laws and norms got him a reputation of brute and unmannered, yet ambitious, cunning, and strong-willed, a person who wouldn't stop in front of anything to achieve his goals. However, history would have remembered him differently, had he been kept accountable for his disregard to the law and his empire collapsed under the brunt of litigation and fines. So, was he a brave, savvy, and defiant businessman, or was he a greedy and corrupted capitalist? Very often, it is a matter of perspective.

All Coming Together

Greed can only be judged from a comparative perspective. It is not intrinsically good or bad. In limited quantities, it can be beneficial to our own development and the progress of the wider society. As they say – everything in moderation. For most of us, greed is merely a motivation to keep pushing and do something better if we want more. Most people are greedy to some extent, as greed has both biological and psychological foundations.

It is undeniable that, taken to extreme levels, greed can ruin individual lives or, in some cases companies, communities, and whole economies. Again, this is not a chapter in defence of greed. In consonance with the spirit of the whole book, the only point I am trying to convey is that most of us have it in us, albeit to varying degrees. There are, of course, many exceptions to the rule - people like medical, police, and academic staff, who have devoted their lives for the greater good of society. These people deserve our utmost respect, but they are an exception, not the rule.

The real problem starts when greed takes over our world and becomes the sole purpose in life. It leads to a soulless and alienated existence, where money is our one and only God. I have spent quite a lot of time looking into various examples where greed results in breaking laws and damaging the lives of others at some extreme level. But these are just some extreme examples. We do not need to take bribes or go to prison to see that many of us have some of it in ourselves.

Yet, few people openly talk about their material desires. It is a fire that keeps burning inside but never to be let out. I will be the first person to raise my hand and admit that I like money. I don't like money for what it is. Holding a piece of paper in my hand gives me no satisfaction whatsoever. But, I certainly like being able to take my fiancé on a nice holiday. I like looking good in some nice new clothes. I like having a Costa or Starbucks coffee from time to time. I like the idea of providing a good home and education for my kids one day. Can I stay at home, instead of going on a holiday? Yes, I can.

Can I drink homemade coffee all the time (I usually do)? Yes, I can. Can I wear my old clothes? Yes, I can. My existence is not predicated on these basic necessities, so if I want an upgrade, this is driven by greed, not need. But this is me - a greedy, primal human being. Am I the only one? Doubt it.

25

Conclusion

More commonly known as Madam C.J. Walker, Sarah Breedlove was born in 1867 in a family of former slaves. He was the first of the family's children to be born free. As you would have guessed now, she did not have it easy. She was orphaned at the age of seven and had to work from a young age. By 14, she was married, and by 20, she was widowed and with a daughter of her own. She then had to work as a laundress and as a cook to send her daughter to school. Things started improving when she got a job as an agent for hair-restoring products. She then branched out and set up her own company in the same field. Despite all these hardships and the tumultuous phases, but due to her resilience and acumen, she went down in history as the first self-made millionaire black woman[90].

The German physicist, Max Planck, was born in 1858. Planck had a natural flair for music. He took singing lessons, played several musical instruments, and composed songs and operas. Despite this, he chose to study physics, which he had an avid interest in. At the University of Munich, his physics professor Philipp von Jolly advised Max against going into physics with the words, "In this field, almost everything is already discovered, and all that remains is to fill a few holes.[91]" This didn't stop Max, and a few years later, he originated the quantum theory, for which he won a Nobel Prize.

Witold Pilecki was a Polish soldier and resistance leader during World War II. His name is lesser-known compared to some of the high-ranking political and military leaders during the war, but Pilecki did something that most people would deem supremely outlandish – he let himself be captured and sent to Auschwitz... on purpose. In 1940, Auschwitz was a big unknown for the allied forces, people were going in but no one was going out. Pilecki was determined to change this and without regard for his safety, he broke curfew and was sent to Auschwitz. During his time there, he managed to organise resistance and intelligence network inside the camp, send information to the outside world regarding the camp's plan, tortures, and conditions inside, and keep the morale of his fellow inmates. He managed to escape in 1943 but continued working with the Polish resistance and cooperated with the allied forces[92].

Stephen King is undeniably one of the most distinguished and successful writers in modern times, maybe in history. But that wasn't always the case. He married his wife in 1971, also a writer, but lived in a trailer while they were both struggling with their careers and were forced to work multiple side jobs to make ends meet. They even had to borrow clothes for their own wedding. King faced more than sixty rejections for his writing before he sold his first story, *The Glass Door,* for $35. Throughout the 70s and 80s, he struggled with alcohol and drugs problems. Today, his books have sold more than 350 million copies worldwide[93].

These are just some examples of the millions of extraordinary people, which have left their mark on the world in one way or another. If we look throughout history, we will find countless examples of people who have completed exceptional feats, done the unthinkable, or somehow shaped the world as we know it today. Now, you may argue that these examples seem contradictory to the general feel of this book. But let me tell you that's not the case. Throughout this book, I have focused on the human side of things, on those traits of our characters, which invariably stand in the way of success or happiness. However, these and many more examples in world history, demonstrate why we have become the most dominant species of all in this world – we are incredible beings, capable of extraordinary actions and achievements, despite our shortcomings.

None of these people stands in contrast to anything I have written to this point because they have succeeded despite the "problems" I have described. None of them got to where they were because they were perfect, not because they have not failed, not because they have not had periods of weakness, not because their actions have always been rational, not because they have not been susceptible to all feelings and emotions that make us human. They have succeeded despite all of this because they persevered, because they kept on going, pushing, seeing beyond their own fallibility.

We live in challenging times. Not because of COVID-19. This will come and pass like many other things in life. I say that because I feel we live in the most demanding of times. Technology, social media, and marketing are major factors that have changed the world beyond recognition in the last few decades. They have presented countless opportunities but also severe challenges. In many ways, we are better off than any of our preceding generations, but we are crippled by pressures to conform, competition on every level, and the pressures of the modern way of life. The problem comes when global trends and tendencies drive us towards convergence of wants, desires, and lifestyles across a diverse population with countless differences in culture, abilities, and socioeconomic means. We are undoubtedly a resilient bunch, but our brains are the result of millions of years of evolution. Their wiring is made for different, simpler worlds, not necessarily fit to face all challenges of modern life. We are made to often act in self-interest, worry about our ego and how we appear to others, have feelings and emotions, which get in the way of rational thought, want more, and make mistakes. We are neither the result of nature nor nurture. We are a combination of both, which makes us who we are. Yet, we expect ourselves and others to act logically, rise above the vain, simple, and material, change our understandings and perceptions to fit the modern world overnight, have strong willpower, and always do the right things... effectively to go against our humanness. Maybe one day we will, as like I said, we are capable of extraordinary feats.

The reason why I started writing this book is not because I am a nihilist or a cynic, who aims to illuminate our shortcomings and discredit our potential for greatness. I am doing it because I believe we are capable of a lot but I wanted to introduce a little note of realism, to help manage our expectations towards ourselves and those around us. We constantly look up to people who have succeeded in one way or another and try to keep up. We want to be everything we can be. We and society expect women these days to be devoted mothers and wives while having successful careers, and staying fit and pretty like the models they put on the magazine covers. There is incredible pressure for women to look good, and society constantly judges them on looks. At the same time, we expect men to be devoted fathers and husbands, be at the top of their earning potential, remain in a good shape, and be fully supportive of everyone else. We expect our kids to do well at school while taking private foreign language lessons, and also do a sport or two. Then we all want to have free time for friends and family, while also having enough money for the latest tech and holidays, do better than everyone else, have successful careers, act smart, and excel at everything. I have some news for you. We cannot. No wonder we have mountains of debt, the income inequality in the world is the highest it has been, and there have been alarming trends in the levels of depression, especially among the younger part of the population.

All I am trying to say with this is that we need to be mindful of our own shortcomings and faults, and factor those in our world expectations. We are not perfect, and we will never be. But we are not born to be perfect, we are born to be human, with all the good and bad that comes with it.

26

Notes

I hope you have enjoyed reading this book. While I am only an amateur in psychology, I developed an interest in the area back at university, when I realised the human element behind a lot of the marketing theory I was studying as part of my business degree. Since then, I have read a significant amount of literature on the topic, but I also spend a lot of time analysing my behaviour and others around me. While we are all unique personalities and no two people are exactly the same in the world, it is a fact that we are all subjected to similar influences, and our behaviours significantly converge.

A lot, if not all, of the topics covered in this book are picked based on my own experiences and observations of myself and the world. They reflect my own views and perceptions, but I have tried to back these up and explain them through established psychological theories. So, while I could be wrong in certain views of mine in some cases, there will be a significant body of reputable information in this book.

It is also prudent to note that I have used many generalisations throughout the book when describing human behaviour. This is inevitable but useful when inferring general tendencies and approaches. Many exceptions apply. There could also be significant cultural variations, which might not necessarily fit every behaviour, covered throughout the book. As I mentioned, many of the behaviours described are from my own experiences and observations, having grown up and lived in Europe my whole life. It is only normal, that I might have a European/Western outlook of the world. Additionally, a lot of the data, theories, and experiments referenced in this book, originate from Western European/American scholars and institutions to the same effect.

If you have learned anything from the chapter on forming and changing attitudes, it should go without saying that my views expressed could be significantly biased based on my life experiences, upbringing, and cultural exposure. All the aforementioned factors need to be considered when reading this book and all information taken with a pinch of salt, despite my conscious effort to stay objective and use credible evidence to back up my ideas. As a human, after having undergone various influences, emotions, and subjective experiences, I must have undoubtedly failed in certain cases.

Finally, I would like to thank my amazing, now wife - Alison, my family, friends, and everyone who has contributed to this book by bouncing off ideas with me and helping to make this book better. I thank you too for taking the time in your undoubtedly busy life to read this book. I will finish with one quote from the 17th century French poet and journalist Anatole France, which perfectly sums up this book – "It is human nature to think wisely and act foolishly."

References

1. Buchholz, K. (no date) Toilet paper producers rolling in the dough, Statista.com. Available at: https://www.statista.com/chart/21327/rise-in-revenue-toilet-paper-selected-countries/ (Accessed: June 6, 2021).
2. Asmelash, L. (2020) "This online toilet paper calculator will tell you just how long your supply will last," CNN, 21 March. Available at: https://www.cnn.copredictablym/2020/03/21/us/toilet-paper-calculator-coronavirus-trnd/index.html (Accessed: June 6, 2021).
3. Legalandgeneral.com. Available at: https://www.legalandgeneral.com/investments/investment-content/how-much-do-brits-really-save/ (Accessed: June 6, 2021).
4. Credit Connect, Almost 5m consumers head into 2020 with personal debts over £10,000, Credit-connect.co.uk. Available at: https://www.credit-connect.co.uk/consumer-news/banking-and-loans/almost-5m-consumers-head-into-2020-with-personal-debts-over-10000/ (Accessed: June 6, 2021).

5. DeGroot, N., Kramer, T. and Wechter, D. (2020) 100 Humans. United States: Netflix.
6. Thaler, R. (1985) "Mental Accounting and Consumer Choice," Marketing science, 4(3), pp. 199–214.
7. Jones, L. (2020) "Coronavirus: What's behind the great toilet roll grab?," BBC, 26 March. Available at: https://www.bbc.co.uk/news/business-52040532 (Accessed: June 6, 2021).
8. Ainslie, G. (2016) "The cardinal anomalies that led to behavioral economics: Cognitive or motivational?: The cardinal anomalies that led to behavioral economics," Managerial and decision economics: MDE, 37(4–5), pp. 261–273.
9. Loewenstein, G., Read, D. and Baumeister, R. F. (2003) Time and decision: Economic and psychological perspectives of intertemporal choice. Edited by G. Loewenstein, Daniel Read, and R. F. Baumeister. Russell Sage Foundation Publications. Available at: https://play.google.com/store/books/details?id=tAO-GAwAAQBAJ.
10. Holiday, R. (2016) Ego is the enemy. Portfolio.
11. Little et al. (2016) "I wore the juice"- the dunning-Kruger effect, Medium. Available at: https://medium.com/@littlebrown/i-wore-the-juice-the-dunning-kruger-effect-f8ac3299eb1 (Accessed: June 8, 2021).
12. Buunk, B. P. and Van Yperen, N. W. (1991) "Referential comparisons, relational comparisons, and exchange ori-

entation: Their relation to marital satisfaction," Personality & social psychology bulletin, 17(6), pp. 709–717.
13. Heck, P. R., Simons, D. J. and Chabris, C. F. (2018) "65% of Americans believe they are above average in intelligence: Results of two nationally representative surveys," PloS one, 13(7), p. e0200103.
14. Fehlhaber, K. and ThemeGrill (2017) The consequences of illusory superiority, Knowingneurons.com. Available at: https://knowingneurons.com/2017/02/06/illusory-superiority/ (Accessed: June 8, 2021).
15. "Leon Festinger - Cognitive dissonance" (no date) Encyclopedia Britannica.
16. Goel, M. (2020) The 'Birther' Movement & ruckus over Kamala Harris' eligibility, Thequint.com. Available at: https://www.thequint.com/explainers/barack-obama-to-kamala-harris-what-is-the-birther-movement (Accessed: June 12, 2021).
17. Festinger, L. (1962) "Cognitive Dissonance," Scientific American, 207(4), pp. 93–106.
18. Berglas, S., & Jones, E. E. (1978). Drug choice as a self-handicapping strategy in response to noncontingent success. Journal of Personality and Social Psychology, 36(4), 405–417
19. Leary, M. R.; Shepperd, J. A. (1986). "Behavioral self-handicaps versus self-reported handicaps: A conceptual note". Journal of Personality and Social Psychology. 51 (6): 1265–1268.

20. Elliot, A. J.; Church, M. A. (2003). "A motivational analysis of defensive pessimism and self-handicapping". Journal of Personality. 71 (3): 369–396.
21. Hartono, W. S. (2018) Judging a book by its cover, Medium. Available at: https://medium.com/@WilliamStefan/judging-a-book-by-its-cover-4813096ad0d9 (Accessed: June 12, 2021).
22. Tyrrell, J. et al. (2016) "Height, body mass index, and socioeconomic status: mendelian randomisation study in UK Biobank," BMJ (Clinical research ed.), 352, p. i582.
23. Gladwell, M. (2006) Blink: The power of thinking without thinking. Harlow, England: Penguin Books.
24. Hollier, R. (2017) Physical attractiveness bias in the legal system — the law project, Com.au. The Law Project. Available at: https://www.thelawproject.com.au/insights/attractiveness-bias-in-the-legal-system (Accessed: June 12, 2021).
25. Implicit Association Test. Harvard.edu. Available at: https://implicit.harvard.edu/implicit/takeatest.html (Accessed: June 12, 2021)
26. Pager, D., Western, B. and Bonikowski, B. (2009) "Discrimination in a low-wage labor market: A field experiment," American sociological review, 74(5), pp. 777–799.
27. Leiber, M. J. and Fox, K. C. (2005) "Race and the impact of detention on juvenile justice decision making," Crime and delinquency, 51(4), pp. 470–497.

28. Friedman, C. (2020) "The relationship between disability prejudice and disability employment rates," Work (Reading, Mass.), 65(3), pp. 591–598.
29. Honoré, B. E. and Hu, L. (2020) The COVID-19 pandemic and Asian American employment. Federal Reserve Bank of Chicago.
30. Britain, L. I. N. (no date) HATE CRIME AND DISCRIMINATION, Org.uk. Available at: https://www.stonewall.org.uk/system/files/lgbt_in_britain_hate_crime.pdf (Accessed: June 12, 2021).
31. Payne, B. K., Vuletich, H. A. and Brown-Iannuzzi, J. L. (2019) "Historical roots of implicit bias in slavery," Proceedings of the National Academy of Sciences of the United States of America, 116(24), pp. 11693–11698.
32. Henry Ford (no date) Wikiquote.org. Available at: https://en.wikiquote.org/wiki/Henry_Ford (Accessed: June 13, 2021).
33. Swaminathan, N. (2008) "Why does the brain need so much power?," Scientific American, 29 April. Available at: https://www.scientificamerican.com/article/why-does-the-brain-need-s/ (Accessed: June 13, 2021).
34. Jones, C. R.; Olson, M. A.; Fazio, R. H. (2010). "Evaluative Conditioning: The "How" Question". Adv Exp Soc Psychol. 43 (1): 205–255.
35. Delventhal, S. (2020) What Nike's $1 billion Ronaldo deal means (NKE), Investopedia.com. Available at: https://www.investopedia.com/news/what-

nikes-1-billion-deal-ronaldo-means/ (Accessed: June 13, 2021).

36. Fetzer, J. S. (2011) "The Evolution of Public Attitudes toward Immigration in Europe and the United States, 2000-2010." Available at: http://dx.doi.org/ (Accessed: June 13, 2021).

37. Olson, J. M. et al. (2001) "The heritability of attitudes: a study of twins," Journal of personality and social psychology, 80(6), pp. 845–860.

38. Segal, N. (1999) Entwined lives: Twins and what they tell us about human behavior. New York, NY: E P Dutton.

39. EURO RSCG; TNS Sofres. (May 2005). "European Values" (PDF). Archived from the original (PDF) on 2007-06-19. Retrieved 2007-06-17. (associated article Archived 2007-09-29 at the Wayback Machine)

40. Author, N. (2006) Spirit and power - A 10-country survey of Pentecostals, Pewforum.org. Available at: https://www.pewforum.org/2006/10/05/spirit-and-power/ (Accessed: June 13, 2021).

41. Sherman, D. K., & Cohen, G. L. (2006). The psychology of self-defense: Self-affirmation theory. In M. P. Zanna (Ed.) Advances in experimental social psychology, 38, pp. 183-242. New York, NY: Guildford Press.

42. Kappes, A. et al. (2020) "Confirmation bias in the utilization of others' opinion strength," Nature neuroscience, 23(1), pp. 130–137.

43. The psychology of willpower: Training the brain for better decisions (2016) Positivepsychology.com. Available at: https://positivepsychology.com/psychology-of-willpower/ (Accessed: June 13, 2021).
44. Baumeister, R. F.; Bratslavsky, E.; Muraven, M.; Tice, D. M. (1998). "Ego depletion: Is the active self a limited resource?" (PDF). Journal of Personality and Social Psychology. 74 (5): 1252–1265.
45. Psychology Today (no date) "How many decisions do we make each day?" Available at: https://www.psychologytoday.com/gb/blog/stretching-theory/201809/how-many-decisions-do-we-make-each-day (Accessed: June 13, 2021).
46. Baumeister, R. F. et al. (1998) "Ego depletion: Is the active self a limited resource?," Journal of personality and social psychology, 74(5), pp. 1252–1265.
47. Yoo, S.-S. et al. (2007) "The human emotional brain without sleep--a prefrontal amygdala disconnect," Current biology: CB, 17(20), pp. R877-8.
48. Adams, C. E. and Leary, M. R. (2007) "Promoting self–compassionate attitudes toward eating among restrictive and guilty eaters," Journal of social and clinical psychology, 26(10), pp. 1120–1144.
49. McGonigal K. (2012) The Willpower Instinct. Daiwashobo.
50. Craig, W. (2001). Enemy at the gates: The battle for Stalingrad. Harlow, England: Penguin Books.

51. Balasa, V. (2013) Failure is feedback: How 5 billionaires had to fail to succeed, Hongkiat.com. Available at: https://www.hongkiat.com/blog/fail-to-succeed-billionaires/ (Accessed: June 13, 2021).
52. Watkins, B. (2019) Thomas Edison's theorem for success - CRY magazine - medium, CRY Magazine. Available at: https://medium.com/cry-mag/thomas-edisons-theorem-for-success-b96591bf7dd1 (Accessed: June 13, 2021).
53. Redburn (2019) Redburn and PWC study finds global marketing industry larger than current estimates. Available at: https://www.redburn.com/wp-content/uploads/2019/01/190129-BTL-Press-Release.pdf (Accessed: July 17, 2021).
54. Festinger, L. (1954). A theory of social comparison processes. Human Relations; Studies towards the Integration of the Social Sciences, 7(2), 117–140.
55. Carlsson, F., Johansson-Stenman, O., & Martinsson, P. (2007). Do you enjoy having more than others? Survey evidence of positional goods. Economica, 74(296), 586–598.
56. Maslow, A. H. (1943). A theory of human motivation. Psychological Review, 50(4), 370–396.
57. Lyall, L. M., Wyse, C. A., Graham, N., Ferguson, A., Lyall, D. M., Cullen, B., … Smith, D. J. (2018). Association of disrupted circadian rhythmicity with mood disorders, subjective wellbeing, and cognitive function:

a cross-sectional study of 91 105 participants from the UK Biobank. The Lancet. Psychiatry, 5(6), 507–514.
58. Hunt, M. G., Marx, R., Lipson, C., & Fomo, Y. J. N. (2018). Limiting social media decreases loneliness and depression. J Soc Clin Psychol, 2018;37(10):751-768, 1521.
59. Tandoc, E. C., Ferrucci, P., & Duffy, M. (1016). Facebook use, envy, and depression among college students: Is facebooking depressing? Comput Hum Behav, 43(139–146), 053.
60. Pearson, E. (2021, March 25). Yuri Gagarin: the first human in space. Retrieved July 17, 2021, from Skyatnightmagazine.com website: https://www.skyatnightmagazine.com/space-missions/yuri-gagarin-first-human-in-space/
61. Why Children of Alcoholics end up Marrying Alcoholics. (2019, September 30). Retrieved July 17, 2021, from Elephantjournal.com website: https://www.elephantjournal.com/2019/09/why-children-of-alcoholics-end-up-marrying-alcoholics-matt-salis/
62. de Berker, A., Rutledge, R., Mathys, C. et al (2016). Computations of uncertainty mediate acute stress responses in humans. Nat Commun 7, 10996
63. Kahneman, D., & Tversky, A. (1979). Prospect theory: An analysis of decision under risk. Econometrica, 47, 263-291.

64. Inesi, M. (2010). "Power and Loss aversion." Organizational Behavior and Human Decision Processes, 112, 58–69
65. Wang, M., Rieger, M. O., & Hens, T. (2016). The Impact of Culture on Loss aversion. Journal of Behavioral Decision Making,30(2), 270-281.
66. Sobieczky, H. (2014). New Design concepts for high speed air transport. New York, NY: Springer.
67. Francis, G. (2018, March 4). Six in 10 British people are afraid of taking risks, study finds. Independent. Retrieved from https://www.independent.co.uk/lifestyle/ afraid-risks-adventure-safety-cautious-people-uk-survey-study-a8238971.html
68. Gigerenzer, G. (2006). Out of the frying pan into the fire: behavioral reactions to terrorist attacks. Risk Analysis: An Official Publication of the Society for Risk Analysis, 26(2), 347–351.
69. Kuhnen, C. M., & Chiao, J. Y. (2009). Genetic determinants of financial risk taking. PloS One, 4(2), e4362.
70. Dharan, B. G., & Bufkins, W. R. (2008). Red flags in Enron's reporting of revenues & key financial measures. SSRN Electronic Journal. doi:10.2139/ssrn.1172222
71. GDP (current US$). (n.d.). Retrieved July 17, 2021, from Worldbank.org website: https://data.worldbank.org/indicator/ NY.GDP.MKTP.CD?year_high_desc=true

72. Teather, D. (2002, June 18). Enron paid out $681m to top executives. The Guardian. Retrieved from http://www.theguardian.com/business/2002/jun/18/corporatefraud.enron
73. Mayka, L. and Lovón, A. (n.d.). Analysis | How one company's deep web of corruption took down governments across Latin America. Washington Post. [online] Available at: https://www.washingtonpost.com/politics/2019/05/23/how-one-companys-deep-web-corruption-took-down-governments-across-latin-america/
74. Psychology Today. (n.d.). Is Greed Good? [online] Available at: https://www.psychologytoday.com/gb/blog/hide-and-seek/201410/is-greed-good.
75. Rauch, J. (2017, November 24). The psychology of greed. Retrieved July 17, 2021, from Talkspace.com website: https://www.talkspace.com/blog/the-psychology-of-greed/
76. Raghavan, A. (2019, March 24). "greed—I have never had that": Rajat Gupta, Wall Street scammer, returns to drop dimes on Goldman, Preet, and former homie Raj rajaratnam. Retrieved July 17, 2021, from Vanity Fair website: https://www.vanityfair.com/news/2019/03/raj-gupta-wall-street-scammer-returns-to-drop-dime-on-preet-and-raj-rajaratnam
77. Smith, A. (1776). An inquiry into the nature and causes of the wealth of nations. Raleigh, N.C.: Alex Catalogue.
78. Stone, Oliver. Wall Street. Twentieth Century Fox, 1987.

79. Early detection of fraud and corruption in public procurement through technology. (n.d.). Retrieved July 17, 2021, from Worldbank.org website: https://www.worldbank.org/en/events/2020/10/06/early-detection-of-fraud-and-corruption-in-public-procurement-through-technology
80. Fraud costs the global economy over US$5 trillion. (n.d.). Retrieved July 17, 2021, from Crowe.com website: https://www.crowe.com/global/news/fraud-costs-the-global-economy-over-us$5-trillion
81. Overview. (n.d.). Retrieved July 17, 2021, from Unodc.org website: https://www.unodc.org/unodc/en/money-laundering/overview.html
82. Hinchliffe, R. (2020, October 22). Three major US banks make up half of 2020's $11.39bn fine total - FinTech Futures. Retrieved July 17, 2021, from Fintechfutures.com website: https://www.fintechfutures.com/2020/10/three-major-us-banks-make-up-half-of-2020s-11-39bn-fine-total/
83. Hinchliffe, R. (2020, October 22). Three major US banks make up half of 2020's $11.39bn fine total - FinTech Futures. Retrieved July 17, 2021, from Fintechfutures.com website: https://www.fintechfutures.com/2020/10/three-major-us-banks-make-up-half-of-2020s-11-39bn-fine-total/
84. Ariely, D. (2008). Predictably irrational: the hidden forces that shape our decisions. New York, NY, Harper.

85. Kale, S. (2019, September 18). One in five of us do it, but is 'wardrobing' ever acceptable? The Guardian. Retrieved from http://www.theguardian.com/fashion/shortcuts/2019/sep/18/is-wardrobing-ever-acceptable-shoppers
86. Graat, M. (2018, January 25). All you need to know about e-commerce returns in Europe. Retrieved July 17, 2021, from Logisticsmatter.com website: https://logisticsmatter.com/need-know-e-commerce-returns-europe/
87. Comparing the cost of retail crime across the UK, US and Europe. (n.d.). Retrieved July 17, 2021, from Retailresearch.org website: https://www.retailresearch.org/crime-comparisons.html
88. Stiles, T. J. (2010). The First Tycoon: The Epic Life of Cornelius Vanderbilt (p. 6). p. 6.
89. Vanderbilt, A. T. (2012). Fortune's Children: The Fall of the House of. Vanderbilt "William Marrow Paperbacks.
90. Dinning, R. (2020, March 18). Self Made: the real story of Madam CJ Walker, America's first black female millionaire. Retrieved July 17, 2021, from Historyextra.com website: https://www.historyextra.com/period/modern/victorian-cj-walker-who-haircare-pioneer-black-woman-millionaire-netflix-self-made-real-history-alelia-bundles-invent/

91. A few holes to fill. (2008). Nature Physics, [online] 4(4), pp.257–257. Available at: https://www.nature.com/articles/nphys921 [Accessed 15 Jan. 2020].
92. Ackerman, E. (2019, July 26). The remarkable story of the man who volunteered to enter Auschwitz and try to tell the world about it. Time. Retrieved from https://time.com/5635746/the-remarkable-story-of-the-man-who-volunteered-to-enter-auschwitz-and-tell-the-world-about-it/
93. LearnVest. (2014, March 27). 9 famous people who will inspire you to never give up. Retrieved July 17, 2021, from Themuse.com website: https://www.themuse.com/advice/9-famous-people-who-will-inspire-you-to-never-give-up

www.ingramcontent.com/pod-product-compliance
Lightning Source LLC
Chambersburg PA
CBHW070920030426
42336CB00014BA/2474